AUTHORING

Authoring

A GUIDE TO THE DESIGN OF INSTRUCTIONAL SOFTWARE

Greg Kearsley

ADDISON-WESLEY PUBLISHING COMPANY, INC.
Reading, Massachusetts   Menlo Park, California
Don Mills, Ontario   Wokingham, England   Amsterdam
Sydney   Singapore   Tokyo   Madrid   Bogotá
Santiago   San Juan

Library of Congress Cataloging-in-Publication Data

Kearsley, Greg, 1951–
   Authoring : a guide to the design of instructional
software.

   Includes index.
   1. Computer-assisted instruction — Authoring
programs.   I. Title.
LB1028.66.K43 1986   371.3'9445   85–28661
ISBN 0–201–11731–2

Cover design by Steve Snider
Text design by Joyce C. Weston
Set in 11 point Caledonia by
Compset Inc., Beverly, MA

ISBN 0–201–11731–2

ABCDEFGHIJ–AL–89876

CONTENTS

PREFACE

"Authoring" is the process of creating instructional software. This book will introduce you to the principles underlying the design of good interactive programs. It covers screen design, user control, response analysis, helps, error handling, and revision. The nature of interactivity and the authoring process are also discussed.

Written primarily for the instructional designer, teacher, or training specialist who is creating computer programs for the first time, this book will also be useful to any software developer or programmer who lacks specific experience designing instructional software.

The guidelines provided in this book apply across all types of instructional applications, all types of computers, and all types of programming languages and systems, because they are based upon the way people learn and think. Regardless of the type of application or computer involved, the rules for designing good instructional software are the same.

This is not a how-to book. It does not tell you the steps to follow in order to create good instructional programs. It is a style guide that tells you what principles to follow and what to avoid. The information here does not cover programming techniques; there are other books available that describe good programming methodology. Nor does it cover curriculum theory or how to use instructional software in the classroom. There are many books on these topics as well (see Appendix).

Many people have made important contributions to this book, including Ron Axtell, Mary Furlong, Robin Halley, Suzanne Sax, Scott Shershow, and David Stone. Special thanks to Bret Wallach and Advanced Processing Laboratories for help in manuscript production and to Wendy Ebersberger, who is a constant source of inspiration and assistance.

San Diego, California
September 1985

AUTHORING

PART 1

Back-
ground

1

INTRODUCTION

This first chapter addresses some important issues in the design of instructional software. These issues include:

☐ computers versus other media
☐ elements of software quality
☐ hardware considerations
☐ programming languages/systems

You do not need to read this chapter or the others in Part 1 if you want to get immediately into the guidelines. However, they provide useful background that may help you understand the guidelines better.

A few words about computer terms and concepts. You do not need any previous acquaintance with computers to use this book. However, familiarity with a certain amount of computer terminology is necessary (e.g., bugs, variables, windows). In order to keep things concise, these terms are used without explanation but are defined in

---

HYPERTEXT: INTERACTIVE DICTIONARIES

In an interactive version of these guidelines, you would be able to touch any word and get an immediate definition in a window at the bottom of the screen. This capability is called "hypertext." The same capability applied to graphic objects produces an explanation of part or all of the graphic you indicate or produces a blow-up of that part of the graphic. In principle, this can be taken to any depth desired (see article by Stone et al. in Appendix).

the Glossary. So, if you run across a word you don't understand, please take a few seconds to look it up in the back of the book.

What are computers good for?

A good place to begin our discussion about the design of instructional software is with the question of when to use computers and when not to use them. Computers are not especially good for presenting a lot of text or graphic information. Print does this much more cheaply, more conveniently, and with better quality. Computers are also not good for presenting a lot of realistic information. Photographic slides or video can do this much more effectively. Video is best for showing dynamic sequences. Finally, computers are not good for activities that require face to face contact. Meetings (or video conferencing) are best for this.

Computers are good for any educational activity that requires a lot of interaction or responses. Games and simulations are probably the best example. In a game or simulation, you must make hundreds of responses, often in a very short time period. Any situation where you are going to answer or ask a lot of questions (e.g., tests, questionnaires, practice exercises, drills, tutorials) is also a good application of computers. Not only can the computer provide immediate feedback or answers to the questions but it can also record the questions and responses. In the context of instruction, this means that the computer can record student performance data.

Computers are also good for providing individualized instruction. Depending upon what responses a student makes to a question or what choices they make in a simulation, they may receive a totally different instructional sequence than another student who makes different responses. For any course that involves students with diverse backgrounds or ability levels, computer-based instruction can be very worthwhile.

Computers are especially good for explaining complex processes and interactions. For example, suppose you are trying to learn or teach the basic principles of harmonic motion, how to change a bicycle tire, why it rains after a hot summer day, the steps in photosynthesis, or the causes of World War I. Through the use of animation and graphics, as well as the capability to change the value of variables and observe the effects, instructional software can have very powerful explanatory value.

Of course, computers are also good for applications such as creating documents (word processing), calculations (spreadsheets), information retrieval (database management), communications (electronic messaging), and controlling other machines (robotics). All of these applications have a major role to play in education and training. Applications software is most often used to teach problem-solving or decision-making skills.

These remarks should give you a perspective for the guidelines outlined in the rest of the book. Computers have unique features that should be exploited in the design of instructional software. They should not be used to mimic the things that other media do better. Screens should not be designed like printed pages and animation should not be used as a substitute for video sequences. Most important, instructional software should be highly interactive. Otherwise, why bother to use a computer?

Elements of software quality

One of the critical skills needed by a software designer is the ability to distinguish a good program from a bad one. Actually, evaluation skills and design skills are mirror images of each other. If you know the elements that result in a well-designed program, you also know the criteria to use in evaluating the quality of programs. In this section, we will briefly discuss the elements of software quality.

Table 1.1 lists some major dimensions of good instructional software. In the context of instruction, a program is sound if it teaches the skills or knowledge it claims to. Usability is measured in terms of the amount of time required to learn how to use a program and the number of mistakes or errors made by the user. A program that has high usability will take very little time to learn and will result in few

Table 1.1   *Good Instructional Software Is:*

Sound	Content is accurate/valid
Usable	Minimal learning time and errors
Motivating	User is involved
Visually Stimulating	Captures attention
Flexible	User in control
Reliable	Consistent and free of bugs
Useful	Something is accomplished

errors. Motivation is a very important characteristic for instructional programs. If a program is motivating, the student will be interested in learning and probably enjoy it.

Because computers are a highly visual medium, it is important that screen displays be visually stimulating. Stimulating displays will capture attention and facilitate learning. To allow users to tailor the program to their needs and interests, the program must offer a lot of flexibility of pace and sequencing. It is imperative that the user have ample control of the program. A program must be very reliable in order to be trusted and believed. This means that it must be consistent in the way it works and be free of bugs. Finally, a program must be useful to the student, i.e., they must feel that they have learned from it.

It is important to note that quality is incremental in nature rather than all or none. One program is better than another because it includes more aspects of good design. In other words, good design means paying attention to lots of different things. There is no single feature or characteristic that produces "quality." Each element makes a contribution. Of course, some features are more significant or noticeable than others.

Of mice and machines

This book does not deal with any specific brand of computer, nor does that matter much from a design viewpoint. The guidelines provided herein apply to any type of machine in the same way that good construction techniques apply to any type of building or proper engineering methods apply to any type of bridge. If you know how to design good quality instruction for one brand of computer, you will be able to do it for any machine.

What does make a difference are the specific features or capabilities of the computer you want to design for. For example, if the computer has a color graphics display, then you are going to be interested in design principles for color and graphics. Similarly, if it features touch input or speech output, you will be interested in the design aspects of these features. Table 1.2 lists some of the specific machine characteristics that have design implications.

One of the problems that you are likely to encounter is that the machine you are designing for has *options*. On many personal computers, the user decides whether to have a monochrome or color display. To the extent that you are designing programs for a machine

Table 1.2   *Machine Features with Design Implications*

Color	How many colors?
Resolution	How much detail can be displayed?
Graphics	What kind of drawings are possible?
Cursor Control	How precisely can things be located?
Function Keys	How many are available?
Video Output	Will videotape/-disc be used?
Memory (RAM)	How much space is available?
Speech I/O	How many words/What quality?
Multi-user	What can/will be shared?

that only comes in one configuration, your job is much easier. For example, all Apple® Macintosh™ machines have the same built-in graphics display, a mouse, and a well-defined software interface incorporating icons and pop-up menus. On the other hand, with IBM PCs, users are likely to have different monitors, input devices, operating systems, and memory configurations.

What do you do as a designer when you don't know what options and capabilities a user will have on his or her computer? You have three logical choices:

1. Design for the minimum configuration of the machine (e.g., monochrome display, minimum memory).
2. Design for a machine with a specific set of features (e.g., color graphics with a certain amount of memory) and make it clear to the user that your program requires this configuration.
3. Design for multiple configurations of a machine. In other words, design your program so that it can be used with a monochrome or color display, with or without touch input, etc.

Clearly, which of these alternatives you choose depends upon the context of your development effort. If you are developing a program for internal use in your school or organization, you may know the characteristics of the machines it will be used on. In this case, choice 2 or 3 is possible. If you were developing a program for commercial sale, you might opt for choice 1 or 3, since you want the program to run on as many machines as possible.

While choice 3 is the most general solution, it is also the most expensive since in most cases you will need to create somewhat different programs for different configurations. On the other hand, choice 1 is the safest and least expensive solution, but one that does not take full advantage of the features that are possible with the machine. Choice 2 is also safe in the sense that you are going to specify exactly features the user's machine must have.

Actually, things are somewhat more complicated than we have discussed so far. In addition to the hardware features listed in Table 1.2, the particular system software in use can also make a difference. For example, with most standard operating systems, a personal computer is not capable of graphics capabilities such as icons, pop-up menus, and overlapping windows. However, with a system manager such as GEM (Digital Research) or Top view (IBM), these kind of capabilities are possible. So, in addition to worrying about different hardware configurations, you also have to take software into account.

To summarize this discussion about machine dependencies, the particular brand or type of computer does not matter from a design point of view. However, the possible configurations of the machine you design programs for may have important implications.

What about programming languages?

This book does not deal with any specific programming language that might be used to create an instructional program. From a design point of view, it does not matter what programming language or authoring system (see discussion below) is used. Just as a writer does not normally know or care how a book is typeset, printed, and bound, you don't need to know or care how a program you have authored is programmed, debugged, tested, and duplicated.

Of course, you may be curious about the implementation process and you may want to learn how to do it yourself. In that case, you will need to deal with a specific programming language or authoring system. The programming step is beyond the scope of this book, but the Appendix provides some recommended readings about programming style.

Many people believe that the selection of a particular programming language or authoring system makes the difference between a good and bad program. This is like believing that with the right pen, you or I could write like Shakespeare or Steinbeck, with the right tennis racquet, we could play tennis like Jimmy Connors or Billie Jean King, with the right piano, we could play like Mozart or Elton John, etc.

The point is that the design of good quality software is a function of teaching experience, knowledge of the subject matter, creative talent, and, of course, a good understanding of design principles for interactive programs. It is not a function of the particular language or system used to create the program.

The language or system does make a difference in how hard or easy it will be to implement a certain design. While virtually any language or system can be used to create any program, in some cases it is so time-consuming or cumbersome that it is not practical to do so. For example, a design may call for illustrations that require a long time to create using the graphics capabilities of a certain programming language/system. In this case, it is possible to do the graphics but would take more time and effort than is reasonable.

In other cases, things specified in the design may not be possible with certain languages or systems. For example, many languages and systems do not provide the capability to display different type sizes or fonts. Some languages do not allow you to create complex graphics (i.e., illustrations) or animation, use a full range of color/shading, produce certain sound effects, accept pointing responses, etc.

It is important to realize that how long it takes to program something is not only a consequence of the specific capabilities of the software, but also a function of the programmer's skill and experience. A very experienced programmer can accomplish things that would take a less experienced programmer much longer to do (or could not do at all). In many cases, the experience level of the programmer is much more significant than the particular language used.

To summarize, the design of your program is independent from its implementation. However, it is important to select a programming language or authoring system that will allow your design to be programmed as you have specified. Similarly, it is desirable to select a programmer who has sufficient experience to complete your design in the most expedient manner possible.

About authoring languages and systems

There is a special class of programming languages that have been developed specifically for the creation of instructional software. These languages are called "authoring languages" or "systems." An authoring language contains the kinds of computer instructions that are needed to implement an instructional program.

Table 1.3   *PILOT Commands*

PR:	Define new problem, set parameters
T:	Display text or variables on the screen
GX:	Display a graphic
TS:	Define a window, set colors or text modes
A:	Accept response
M:	Match response
J:	Jump to designated label / last A: or PR: / next M:
W:	Wait specified duration
R:	Remark
C:	Do numeric computation or variable assignment
S:	Generate sounds
U:	Use a subroutine
L:	Link to another program
K:	Store a response
V:	Execute a video control instruction
FI:	Read from a disk file
FO:	Write to a disk file

Table 1.3 lists the commands of PILOT, an authoring language widely used on microcomputers. It includes commands for displaying text (T:, TS:), requesting input (A:), matching responses (M:), branching (J:), calling subroutines (U:), linking to an external program (L:), storing student responses (K:), reading and writing to files (FI:, FO:), making a comment (R:), and assigning variables (C:). Other authoring languages have similar commands.

There are dozens of authoring languages in existence (see Appendix). The major advantage of using an authoring language over a regular programming language (such as BASIC, Pascal, or LISP) is that authoring languages have the specific kinds of capabilities needed to write instructional programs. However, they are programming languages and hence belong in the hands of a programmer. As with any type of programming language, a lot of time for debugging will be needed.

An authoring system, on the other hand, does not involve any actual programming and requires considerably less debugging. Authoring systems are an example of a kind of software called "program generators." They allow anyone to create a program without having to write computer instructions. Instead, you respond to prompt messages, select options from menus, or use simple commands to create your program. You can buy program generators to create screen displays, databases, or expert systems.

There are many authoring systems commercially available. They speed up development time because the debugging step associated with the use of a programming (or authoring) language is minimized. Since debugging can account for as much as 50 percent of the time required to complete a program, this can result in appreciable savings. Furthermore, the use of an authoring system means that you can actually create the program yourself without needing a programmer.

Alas, every silver lining has its cloud. In order for a program generator to work, it must have a well-defined structure. In the case of authoring systems, this means that you will be able to create certain kinds of instructional programs which fit into the structure of the particular authoring system. If you want to do something different or unusual, you will have a hard time. For example, many current authoring systems are designed for tutorial type instruction. It is difficult to use them to create simulations or games. Or they may allow you to use only certain color combinations or lay out screen displays in a particular way.

Some of the more recent authoring systems include an authoring language capability. Such systems provide the efficiency of an authoring system as well as the flexibility of an authoring language. Many authoring systems and languages allow you to link to programs written in other programming languages (e.g., BASIC, Pascal) or use text files created with a word processing program. When selecting an authoring system or language, you should look for these capabilities.

If an authoring system does provide you with sufficient flexibility to create the program as you want, then you should use it to increase your authoring productivity. However, keep in mind the remarks made in the preceding section. Your design is more important than the authoring software used and experience with the authoring software will make a significant difference. Even though an authoring system eliminates the need for programming expertise, experience with the authoring system is still needed to use it well.

In summary, special-purpose authoring software exists to make it faster and easier to develop instructional programs. You should become familiar with this type of software in order to know what capabilities or limitations it presents for your design activities. The Appendix provides some references for further reading.

Summary

Computers are best suited to instructional applications that involve a lot of interaction and explanation of complex processes. Other media (i.e., print, video) are better for the presentation of static or sequential information.

The basic dimensions of software quality are soundness, usability, motivation, visual stimulation, flexibility, reliability, and usefulness. Quality is incremental in nature: the more elements present in a program, the better the quality.

In general, design principles apply across all types of computers. However, different machines permit different kinds of design features (e.g., color, display quality, input modes). A major consideration is that the same machine may have many options in terms of display, memory, or input/output devices.

A variety of programming languages and authoring systems are available for creating instructional software. The particular language or system used to develop programs can have substantial impact on the authoring time required. However, the characteristics of the design itself are more important than the specific development software used as far as quality and effectiveness are concerned.

2

THE NATURE OF INTERACTIVITY

As pointed out in the previous chapter, interactivity is the primary basis for using computers in instruction. In this chapter, the nature of interactivity will be explored further. We will look at levels of response, instructional strategies, and ways of presenting interactive sequences.

Levels of response

The kind of interactivity possible can be analyzed in terms of the type of user response made. Table 2.1 lists a series of different levels of response in order of increasing sophistication and associated response processing.

The simplest kind of response is a key press that indicates acknowledgment. For example, the user presses the space bar or the ENTER/RETURN key to see the next screen. The next level of response is a choice from a list of options in a menu or a multiple-choice question. The user chooses a particular response by typing a single letter or number or by moving the cursor to that response. A more complex type of response is a word, phrase, or numerical answer that is typed

Table 2.1

LEVELS OF RESPONSE	RESPONSE PROCESSING REQUIRED
1. Single Key Press / Pointing	Match Key / Position
2. Multiple-Choice Selection	Match Characters / Positions
3. Words, Phrases, Numbers	Keywords, Calculation
4. Multiple Responses	Match Sequence
5. Natural Language / Speech	Parser, Pattern Recognition

in. A response that involves a sequence of responses that must be selected or typed in, represents a more complex response. The most complex type of response is natural language or speech input.

Clearly, the amount of information expressed in a response increases as we change levels. Compare the information in a single key press versus a natural language answer. The complexity of the response processing required also varies with the level of the response as shown on the right side of Table 2.1. Key presses or pointing responses require only single-character or positional matches. Responses consisting of words, phrases, or numeric answers require a series of string matches and introduce problems having to do with misspelling, order, upper/lower case, decimal places, etc. Responses that are expressed in natural language or speech require parsers and pattern recognizers that employ artificial intelligence techniques.

To summarize, interactivity can be defined in terms of the level of response that a program allows. As the level of response increases in complexity, the response processing needed increases correspondingly. In other words, as a program becomes more interactive due to more complex response processing, the design process becomes more lengthy and involved.

Types of instructional strategies

A second way of analyzing interactivity is in terms of different types of instructional strategies that can be used in programs. Table 2.2 lists these strategies in order of increasing design complexity.

Drills and multiple-choice tests constitute the simplest types of instructional strategies. Both involve the presentation of a question or problem followed by a request for a response. Simple helps (i.e.,

Table 2.2   *Instructional Strategies*

Drills
Multiple-Choice Tests
Simple Helps
Tutorials
Adaptive Tests
Applications Programs
Simulations / Games
Context Dependent Helps
Intelligent Tutors / Coaches

fixed format) and tutorials involve a series of presentations and responses. Adaptive tests determine the questions to be presented based upon the pattern of responses. Applications programs such as word processing, database managers, or spreadsheets involve unique response sequences associated with the problem the student is trying to solve using the program. The responses generated in a simulation or game depend upon the previous or successive values specified by the student for parameters or moves. Similarly, the advice provided by a context-sensitive help depends upon the current state of the task and exactly what the user is trying to do. Intelligent coaches and tutors build a model of the user to determine how to respond and handle user responses.

Each of these instructional strategies usually involves an increasingly more sophisticated type of interactivity. The interaction increases in terms of individualization, relevance, and involvement. The questions or problems posed in a drill, and the feedback provided, are not unique. However, the queries posed in a database search or the sequence of events produced in a game or simulation are likely to be one of a kind. Certainly, the interaction created in an intelligent tutor is highly personalized and resembles a conversation between two people.

Increased interactivity also produces a higher degree of student involvement while using the program. Consider the degree of involvement that exists in a good video game or realistic simulation. The user's concentration is very intense and all external distractions are blocked out. The response rate is very high and system response time is very quick.

The design time required for each of these different kinds of instructional strategies increases by orders of magnitude. This is because the number of alternatives to be taken into account and the amount of information needed increases geometrically as the interaction gets more sophisticated. Thus, an adaptive test may take ten times longer to create than a multiple-choice test, or an intelligent tutor may take a hundred times more time to create than a tutorial on the same topic.

Branching is the essence of interactivity

Interactivity is produced by branching within a program. While it is not important that you know how to write a branch instruction, it is important that you understand how branching works. When you design a program, you must be able to specify the logic of the instructional sequence via a flow chart or some other representational scheme. The critical aspect of the logic that you want to describe is the branching structure. In this section, a number of different examples of branching are described.

The first example is a multiple-choice question with three response options. In Figure 2.3 the question and response screens are shown on the left; the logic is shown on the right.

The branching in this example (represented by the diamond-shaped decision box) is the selection of one of the three possible feedback messages. This type of branching structure would be found in any drill, test, or tutorial.

The second example illustrates the kind of branching that would be found in a game or simulation (see Figure 2.4). It involves a variable type of response. Imagine a stickshift that controls the speed of

Figure 2.3

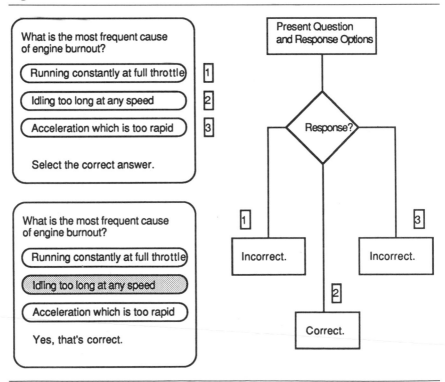

Figure 2.4

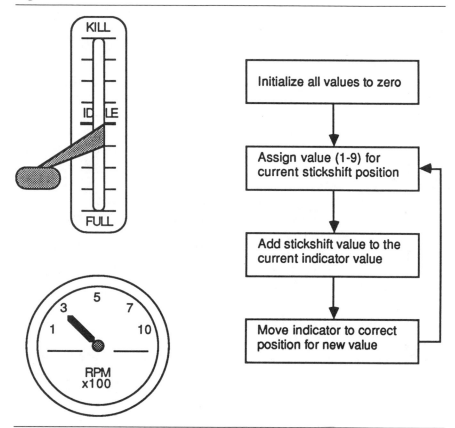

a motor. As the stickshift is moved from the KILL to the FULL throttle position and back, the speed of the motor increases or decreases. Speed is shown by the reading of the dial in revolutions per minute (rpm). The throttle and dial are shown on the left in the figure. The branching structure for this sequence is shown on the right.

The branching logic in Figure 2.4 works as follows. The position (1-9) that the stickshift is moved to by the user is translated into a value between −4 and 4. The IDLE position corresponds to 0. Every second, the indicator on the dial is moved the number of notches given by the value (positive values are forward; negative values are backward). This is the loop shown between the last box and the second box in the flow chart. Since there are four notches for each 100 rpm (not shown on the dial), it would take ten seconds to reach 1,000 rpm if the throttle is put into FULL position. When the stickshift is put in the IDLE position, the value is 0 so the indicator stays at its current position on the dial. Note that in the beginning, the indicator will not start to move until the stickshift is past the idle position. Also note that any rpm value below 0 or above 10 will not move the indicator beyond the initial or final positions on the dial.

The third example of branching is an intelligent coaching segment for a simulation involving the throttle sequence in the preceding example and the diagnostic knowledge of the first example. The purpose of this segment is to detect users who frequently idle and warn them that this may result in engine burnout. The logic for the coach is shown in the flow chart on the right of Figure 2.5. The advice generated by the coach when the problem is detected is shown in the screen on the left of the figure.

Note that the advice is only generated after the idling behavior is shown ten times in a session. Thus, the coach looks for patterns of behavior rather than single responses.

These three examples illustrate differences in branching structures for different response levels and instructional strategies. In the first example, the branching determines which feedback message is displayed and depends upon which answer is selected. In the second example, the branching determines the movement of a dial indicator

Figure 2.5

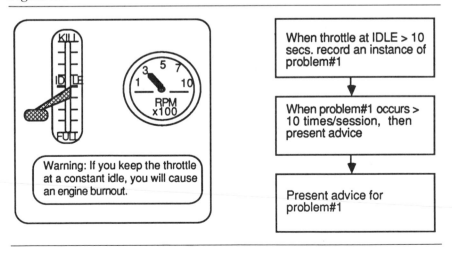

and depends upon the position of the throttle stickshift. In example three, the branching determines when (and if) certain advice is given and depends upon whether the stickshift is kept in an idle position frequently. The branching logic in each successive example is more complex and results in a more sophisticated degree of interactivity.

Using response data

Interaction between people involves an exchange of information. We make inferences and draw conclusions on the basis of the information revealed. A well-designed instructional program does this too. In fact, the recording and use of response data is one of the characteristics of instructional software that distinguishes it from other types of interactive programs.

Every time you make a response when using a computer, it can be recorded. This includes answers to questions as well as any sequence of key presses or pointing actions made. Time durations can also be measured. For example, the time taken to go through a lesson or unit can be recorded and used to estimate the difficulty in understanding the material presented. The time taken to provide an answer to a question (response latency) can also be measured and used to assess how well the person knows the answer.

The response data collected is used to make branching decisions as outlined in the previous section. There are basically three kinds of branching criteria: counters, vectors, and knowledge networks. With counters, a branching decision is made on the basis of the value of a single variable. For example, here is a set of branching rules based upon a counter SCORE which keeps track of the total number of correct answers in a lesson:

> If SCORE < 10 then repeat lesson from beginning
> If SCORE > 10 and < 20 then go to lesson 21
> If SCORE > 20 then go to lesson 24

With vectors, the branching decision is made on the basis of a pattern of responses. For example, suppose the user has just completed a pretest for a course consisting of seven questions, each with three alternatives. The following set of rules might be used to determine what sequence of lessons the person should see based upon their answers to the questions in the pretest:

If answers = {a,c,b,a,a,a,c} then lessons 1,2,3,5,8,9
If answers = {a,c,a,c,b,b,a} then lessons 1,2,3,7,8,9,10
If answers = {b,c,a,a,a,c,a} then lessons 1,3,8,10

Clearly the use of vectors allows for many possible branching paths. In the example just described, there would be over 2,000 possible alternatives (7 questions with 3 choices each). It is likely that only a small subset of these alternatives would have instructional meaning.

With knowledge networks, branching decisions are made on the basis of matching concepts or diagnosing misconceptions. Normally, this will involve natural language understanding capability and the use of artificial intelligence programming techniques. For example, consider the following branching rules that might be found in an intelligent tutoring program on the basic principles of electricity:

If answer = {metal conducts electricity} then go to lesson 5
If answer = {wood conducts electricity} then explain {properties of wood}
If answer = {rubber insulates electricity} then ask about {metal}

In the first rule, if the answer contains the concept that metal conducts electricity, then lesson 5 is started. However, if the answer contains the misconception that wood conducts electricity, then the tutor needs to explain about the electrical properties of wood. If the answer indicates an understanding of the insulating properties of rubber, it is necessary to ask about the properties of metal. Note that natural language understanding capability will be needed to determine if the answers provided match the concepts stated in the rules.

We have been discussing the use of response data for branching. Response data is also important in analyzing the effectiveness of a

---

RESPONSES DON'T ALWAYS NEED TO BE EVALUATED

It is worth noting that user responses don't always need to be evaluated. For example, you might ask the student to make a list of factors that affect something or rate a set of statements. You might count the number of factors listed or summarize the ratings, but there would be no actual evaluation of the responses in terms of predefined answers.

program and deciding what revisions are needed. This will be discussed at length in Chapter 10.

Question answering versus question asking

Historically, the design of instructional software has focused on programs such as drills, tutorials, or simulations which require students to answer questions or specify parameters. In general, these programs have been concerned with achieving comprehension and understanding facts, concepts, or principles. In recent years, the focus has shifted to programs that allow students to ask questions and are more concerned with the student's ability to solve problems, make decisions, or reach conclusions. The increasing popularity of helps, applications programs, and intelligent tutors are good examples of this trend.

For example, consider how application programs are used for instruction. A student may use a graphics or spreadsheet program in order to reach conclusions about the results of a science experiment or business problem. A database program may be used to search for information needed to write a report. A computer-aided design (CAD) program may be used by an engineering student to learn how to design buildings, aircraft, or computer circuits.

This trend toward the use of instructional software for question asking rather than answering has important design implications. Less attention is needed for the design of traditional question formats or branching sequences and more for providing good user control in a program. If a student is going to use a program primarily to ask questions, it is critical that it be easy to do so. Chapter 6 discusses the design of user control.

Instead of being concerned with the evaluation of responses, the emphasis is on the formulation of good questions and problem-solving strategies. For this reason, helps that provide advice or guidance to the student play an especially important role in this type of software. The design of helps is discussed in Chapter 8.

Summary

There are a number of different ways of defining interactivity. Interactivity is a function of the levels of response involved in a program and the instructional strategies used. Different levels of response include single key presses, multiple-choice selections, words or expressions, multiple responses, and natural language/speech input. Different instructional strategies include drills, multiple-choice tests, helps, tutorials, adaptive tests, databases, simulations/games, and intelligent tutors/coaches.

Interactivity is produced by means of branching. Three different examples of branching were examined in this chapter: a multiple-choice question, an indicator controlled by a stickshift, and advice from an intelligent coach.

User responses are the basis for making branching decisions. Three types of decision criteria that can be used for branching are counters, vectors, and knowledge networks.

The trend in instructional software is toward the use of programs that allow students to ask questions rather than just answer them. The design of user control options and helps are important for this type of software.

3

THE AUTHORING PROCESS

This chapter discusses the process of authoring. This includes different types of authoring approaches, the use of design documents, prototypes, and pilot testing. Factors affecting development times are also discussed.

Different approaches to authoring

There are many approaches to creating instructional software. Let's compare two scenarios representing different ends of the authoring spectrum: a college instructor versus a courseware production team.

Our college instructor works as a lone artist, handcrafting the program and making all decisions on the basis of intuition and personal teaching experience. Most of the development is done in the evenings and on weekends; there is no development schedule or target completion date. An authoring system is used to produce completed lessons without any need for programming. The authoring system includes a graphics editor which allows the instructor to draw all graphics. The resulting program is creative, stimulating, and free of bugs.

The courseware production team belongs to a commercial software development company and must turn out good quality programs according to a specification, schedule, and budget. Table 3.1 lists the team composition.

All the team members work on a number of projects simultaneously. The project manager coordinates the work of all the team members and keep the development on schedule and on budget. The team follows well-defined procedures for each step of the development process. The names of some of these procedures are listed in Table 3.2.

The programmer uses a standard programming language to code the program. The graphics designer creates graphics using a graphics

Table 3.1   *Courseware Production Team*

Instructional Designer
Subject Matter Expert
Programmer
Graphics Designer
Script Writer
Editor
Project Manager
Evaluation Specialist

Table 3.2   *Instructional Development Procedures*

Needs/Task Analysis
Objectives Hierarchies
Media Selection
Lesson Specifications
Storyboarding
Prototyping
Tryouts
Field Testing

editor that produces files to be integrated into the program by the programmer. The software undergoes extensive testing and revision. The resulting program is creative, stimulating, and free of bugs.

Despite the major differences between these two development approaches, the resulting programs could be very good (or very bad). The critical factor is not the approach used, but the extent to which the design principles described in the next part of this book are followed. What will determine the quality of the programs produced is whether the single author or the production team has experience designing instructional software.

The two cases just described represent two extremes. Instructional software can be developed by groups of any size and with various backgrounds. Embedded training for applications software may be developed by members of a software engineering group. Individual teachers may develop tests or simulations for use in their classes. Developers at educational software companies may produce drills or games for home computer use. In other words, there is no right or wrong approach to authoring.

Documenting your design

Regardless of what kind of approach is followed, one important aspect of authoring is good documentation of the design. While it is possible to do all authoring directly at the terminal, this is very unlikely given the complexity of instructional software. Furthermore, when working in any kind of team arrangement, or when approval or review of a design is needed, it is necessary to have the program documented in some fashion so its design can be communicated.

Figure 3.3   *Lesson Synopsis*

Lesson Synopsis

Course: *Engines I*   Lesson: *A08*   Author: *WSE*

The purpose of this lesson is to teach the student the major causes of engine burnouts. This includes poor shifting, excessive idling, or red-lining.

The lesson begins with a tutorial which explains these factors. Included in the tutorial are questions which check the student's understanding of the concepts. Wrong answers to the questions provide remedial discussions.

After the student has completed the tutorial, a simulation is provided for practice. The simulation consists of a throttle shifter and a dial showing rpm. The student is prompted to run the engine at certain rpms for specified time intervals to produce engine burnouts.

After the student has completed the simulation, a game is provided which uses the same display with a timer and distance gauge provided. The goal of the game is to go a specified distance in the least amount of time without blowing the engine. A coach provides advice.

Two levels of design documentation are needed: a general (or macro) description, and a detailed (or micro) description. The general design document needs to provide a brief overview or synopsis of the program (see Figure 3.3). More specifically, it needs to describe the purpose and objective(s) of the program, whom it is intended for (what ages or prerequisite skills are assumed), and how the program will work. Someone should be able to read the macro design document in a few minutes and understand the nature of the program.

There are basically three things that need to be described for the detailed design: screen layouts, response processing, and branching logic. A grid is typically used to represent screen layouts. Response processing is shown by indicating the appropriate answer matches and feedback messages. Branching logic is represented by conditional statements (If...then) or flow charts. This information is usually combined in a storyboard. Figure 3.4 shows an example of a storyboard.

One storyboard is completed for each new display or sequence in the program. Each storyboard contains identification information as well as explanatory comments. Storyboards should provide all the design information needed to understand or create an instructional program. They can be used by reviewers to approve or suggest changes to a program before it is actually coded. Storyboards can also

---

SOFTWARE TRANSPORTABILITY

Transportability of software across different systems is a major issue in the instructional domain. After spending a lot of time and money developing a program, it is desirable to have it run on as many different computers as possible. The problem is that a program developed for one machine is not likely to run on a different machine. One solution to this problem is to use programming or authoring languages which are available for a wide variety of machines. However, in many cases, it will be necessary to rewrite the program from the storyboards using a different language or system. In these cases, storyboards play an important role in transportability.

Figure 3.4

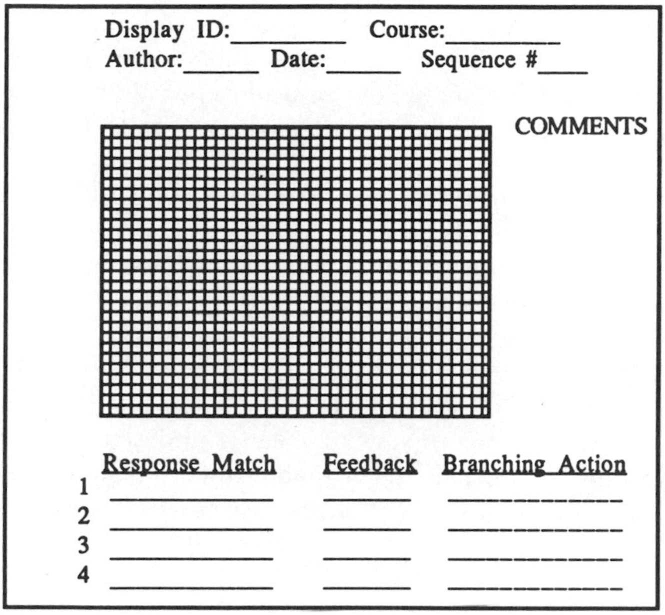

be used to implement the same program on different computers or using different programming software. They represent the machine independent aspect of program design.

The importance of prototypes

While storyboards provide a detailed description of the program, they do not convey the interactive or dynamic aspects very well. It is very difficult to visualize exactly how a program will work from the storyboards. For this reason, it is highly desirable to create prototypes of a program as part of the design step.

A prototype is a working model or mockup of the actual program. It is only a small part of the entire program and usually contains a few representative displays or sequences. While the prototype works, it may not work in the same way as the real program will. For example, a function which graphs data may display a stored graph instead of actually generating one from the input provided, an animation may be represented by a few discrete screens instead of a full sequence, or only some of the feedback messages for a response are implemented. The challenge in building a prototype is to create enough of the program to illustrate how it will work, but do as little actual programming as possible.

Another function of a prototype is to assess how difficult it will be to program certain sequences. It is often difficult to estimate how long it will take to program something that has not been done before. Implementing these sequences in a prototype allows a more accurate estimate of how long the full design will take.

The best way to decide what should go into a prototype is to go through the completed storyboards and select examples of sequences which are very common or very unusual. You may want to include a complete unit or segments from many units. At most, a prototype should contain no more than 10 percent of the entire program.

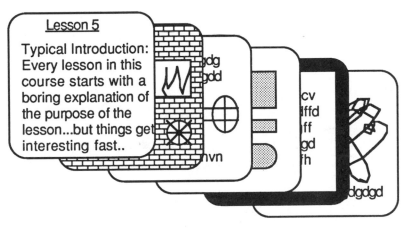

A prototype should contain a sample of everything in the program.

Pilot testing is essential

No matter how well a design was thought out and how carefully it was programmed, there will still be many things that have been overlooked. This includes unexpected responses, missing examples, ambiguous directions, unclear explanations, additional helps that are needed, and so on. The purpose of pilot testing is to discover these flaws.

There are lots of ways to do pilot tests. They can be done as one-on-one tryouts where the evaluator sits with the user and observes the problems that occur. The tryout may be videotaped for detailed analysis after the session. Alternatively, the program can be tested with a group of users who fill out questionnaires after they have completed the tryout. Questionnaires or the capability to make comments can be built into the tryout program so that users can provide feedback as they actually go through it.

While some of these methods provide more detailed or accurate data than others, any form of pilot testing will produce useful information. The more pilot testing you can do the better. Each new person who tries out the program may reveal a problem or weakness that everyone else had missed. Because the only way to get programs bug-free is trial and error, you need lots of trials to find all the errors. Generally, pilot testing should be continued until you run out of time or money.

One of the problems in pilot testing is deciding when to make changes that deal with preferences rather than errors. A simple rule of thumb is: make changes suggested by only one person when they seem like major improvements, give serious consideration to any changes suggested by two different individuals, and always makes changes suggested by three or more people (no matter what you think!). In Chapter 10, we will discuss more formal methods of analyzing response data which can also be used in pilot testing.

A few (hundred) words about development time

One of the most asked questions about the development of instructional software is "How long does it take to develop a program?" This question is analogous to the question "How long does it take to build a house?" Both questions have the same answer: "It depends."

It depends on how fancy you want your program to be, how big, and how fast you want it built. It also depends upon the experience of the author (or authoring team), the extent to which the curriculum already exists in some form, and the authoring tools used. These factors can account for an order of magnitude difference in development time.

Experienced authors may be able to develop a program in half the time required by inexperienced authors (since they are familiar with the guidelines outlined in this book). Some authoring systems can reduce the development time by as much as 40 percent relative to the use of a programming language. If the curriculum already exists in classroom or self-study form, up to 50 percent of the development time may be saved compared to creating the program for a totally new course. If we combine these three time savings, we could theoretically reduce the development time for a program by 90 percent! In practice, some aspects of design (such as quality review and revision) tend to be a constant for a program of a given type and size.

Another factor to keep in mind is that each additional display or presentation feature you use (e.g., windowing, color, graphics, sound, speech, video) will increase the development time and costs (see Figure 3.5). Each feature has to be thought about, programmed, debugged, and tested. The design dilemma is that you can create a simple program quickly or take a lot longer for a fancy one.

The development time depends on the level of quality desired. If a program is to include all of the elements of quality mentioned in Chapter 1, more development time will be required than if only a few are taken into account. An explicit decision about the quality desired for a program is made by specifying what elements will/will not be included.

Figure 3.5

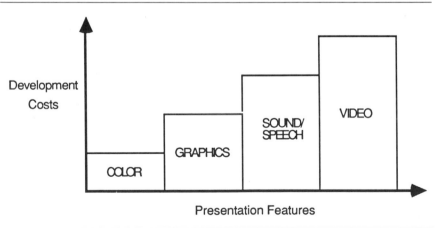

There are some important practical rules that you can derive from the preceding discussion. The development time (and costs) of software will be minimized if you:

1. Use curriculum that already exists in some form
2. Use authors with experience creating instructional software
3. Use the most powerful authoring tools available
4. Use the simplest presentation strategies possible
5. Specify exactly what level of quality is desired

In most situations, you will not have control over all these factors. However, you are likely to have control over some of them and this gives you an opportunity to reduce development time and costs.

Summary

Authoring approaches can range from a single individual doing all aspects of design and development to a team consisting of many members. The experience of the author(s) creating instructional software is the most important factor determining the success of the authoring approach.

Design needs to be documented at two levels: macro and micro descriptions. The macro description is provided by a lesson synopsis. Storyboards for each display or sequence in the program provide the micro description.

Prototypes are important in the design process because they provide a concrete example of what the program will look like and how it will work. A prototype should consist of a sample of critical elements of the program.

Pilot testing is crucial in finding flaws in programs. Pilot tests can be conducted one-on-one or in groups. Data can be collected by observation or by having participants complete online or offline questionnaires. The more pilot testing conducted, the better.

The amount of time required to develop instructional software depends upon a number of factors, including: (1) the experience of the author(s), (2) the extent to which the curriculum already exists, (3) the authoring tools used, (4) the presentation features involved, and (5) the quality desired.

4

INTEGRATING SOFTWARE WITH OTHER MEDIA

One of realities of current instructional software usage is that it is normally used in conjunction with other delivery media. In this chapter we look at the integration of software with print, audio, video, and classroom presentations. This is an important topic because if the integration is not done properly, neither the software nor the associated media may work well.

Probably the most general design rule for mixing software with other media is that it needs to be designed as a single entity. Adding software to existing materials (or vice versa) often results in something analogous to a patchwork quilt. Whenever possible, software and other media should be designed at the same time so they fit together smoothly.

Print media in the form of technical manuals and textbooks represents the most common way to package and distribute instruction. Ironically, print is also the most common format for teaching people how to use software. Print is relatively inexpensive, takes minimum development time/money and is highly flexible. Furthermore, it is a media with which we are all very familiar. Even today, it is much easier to find writers and printing companies than it is to find programmers and software development firms.

Audio- and videocassettes are also commonly used for instruction. Audiocassettes are popular for self-study learning in areas such as interpersonal and business skills, personal health, and foreign languages. Since most people own a cassette player (not to mention stereo), this is a convenient form of presentation. Videocassettes are used for all forms of training by corporations and government agencies. As more and more people come to have videocassette players in their homes, this becomes a viable option for home learning as well.

Videodisc is not widely used at present although it is used in a number of leading edge projects in training and education. It will probably be many years before videodisc becomes as common as audio- or videocassettes. However, it is almost certain to succeed (in one form or another) because of the tremendous storage capability it provides.

Classroom instruction is the most common form of delivering instruction. Approximately 75 percent or more of all formal learning takes place in a classroom setting. For this reason, the use of software in classroom instruction is a significant consideration. At the present time, computers are not used extensively as part of classroom activities, except when the training is about computers.

ELECTRONIC MEDIA

One day all media is likely to be in electronic form. Text, photographs, motion sequences, and graphics will be created/captured and stored digitally. Still and movie cameras will produce digital images. Most class and meeting rooms will have video projectors as they now have overhead projectors. People will also have video projectors in their homes. Audio and speech will also be digitally recorded and stored. Handheld computers will make it easy to create or display anything anywhere. Electronic networks will provide access to remotely located databases. Science fiction or future reality?

Software documentation

The most common combination of print and software are "user guides," which teach someone how to use a particular computer program. The major problem with such documentation is that it presents a linear learning path, whereas people almost never learn how to use a program in a linear fashion. People tend to explore or make mistakes that quickly take them on a different learning path.

This presents a real dilemma to the designer of the documentation. Usually there are some basic functions or operations that users must know before they can use the program or system properly. It makes sense to teach these basics before more advanced capabilities. However, if the user won't follow a linear learning sequence, it is difficult to know how to design the documentation to accommodate prerequisites.

To deal with this problem, the documentation should be designed in very short sections (modules) associated with specific functions or operations. Each section should start independently and not depend upon the outcomes of a previous section. If the user does get hopelessly tangled up in one section, they can start over again or go on to the next section without a problem.

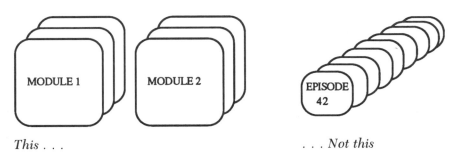

This . . .   *. . . Not this*

When the user is asked to do something, there should be a description of all the likely error conditions as well as the expected result. In other words, the instructions should look this:

> **Now, select the F1 function key to see the updated amount.**
> If you accidently press a different key, press F1 again.
> If pressing F1 doesn't work, press the ESC key and select the RESUME
> option, then press F1.

Clearly, the extent to which you can suggest proper recovery procedures depends upon how the software was designed. Some software makes this difficult because it does not handle errors well (see Chapter 9).

The two most typical problems that users have with software documentation are knowing just when to do something and getting lost after doing something on the system. When people are learning to use a computer, they generally have an action orientation. This means that they will try something as soon as they read about it. In addition, many manuals do not clearly distinguish between describing something and having users try it. This frequently causes a problem because users will try something before it has been properly explained, or they will fail to do something when they are expected to do so. To avoid this problem, it is critical to have a way to distinguish explanations from instructions to do something. This can be achieved by always stating actions as imperatives (e.g., Type the following . . .) and using color, highlighting, italics, or some other cueing technique to signify an action is required.

People frequently get lost after a hands-on activity because they forget where they left off in the documentation. To avoid this problem, it is desirable to place hands-on activities at the end of a module. After completing the activity, users begin a new module rather than try and find their place in the middle of a module. It is also desirable to put some sort of identifier on the screen (e.g., Exercise 4) to remind people where they are. The best aid is a prompt message on the system that tells the user to go back to the documentation and continue reading at a certain page or section. This is an example of how the print and the system need to be designed together in order to work well.

Illustrations of screen displays help users locate themselves and provide confidence that they are on the right track. Good software documentation makes extensive use of screen illustrations. A slight problem with using screen displays is that they tend to change with each different version of the program. However, small discrepancies do not seem to bother users significantly.

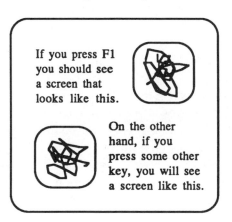

Illustrate documentation with screen displays.

Even the best designed print documentation can only work moderately well because of the way people naturally learn to use computers. Online instruction in the form of helps or embedded tutorials are a much better solution than print. With online instruction, users get exactly the information they need at the moment regardless of what learning path they have taken.

One technique that does allow print documentation to work fairly well is to modify the system so that only the functions currently being discussed are active. Trying to use any function other than the currently active one produces a "Not available at present" message. This eliminates the problem of users going off on different paths. It requires the ability to modify the system to enable and disable functions.

Books

Book/software combinations are just beginning to appear. In general, the print component provides information, while the software provides a diagnostic assessment, financial model, database, or simulation. For example, programs on management skills (e.g., leadership, negotiation, delegation, etc.) present the basic concepts and principles in print and the program permits a self-assessment of these skills. A flight simulation program comes with a manual that explains the basic principles of flying. A book on telecommunications for personal computers provides simulated telecommunications sessions on the diskette. A diskette accompanying a math textbook scores answers and provides remedial feedback for the exercises in the book. A book on wills provides a diskette that will print out your own will once you have filled in the necessary information. A program that accompanies a diet book generates a personalized diet program for the reader.

The distinctive characteristic of all of these applications is that the program takes advantage of the interactive capability of the computer. The programs do not present information; this is best done via print. Instead, they provide capabilities for individualized assessment, simulation, and modeling or customized document preparation.

The software that comes with a book does not have to be as closely coordinated as user manuals and documentation. Usually, it is packaged separately and can be added after the book is written. Software that accompanies a book extends its value and is sometimes called *value-added* software.

Audio- and videocassettes

Software is often used in conjunction with audio- or videocassettes as part of self-study learning packages. This is similar to the use of print and software programs for user documentation. Many of the remarks made under Software Documentation above apply to the design of audio/video packages. Getting lost going between the audio or video activities and software is a frequent problem. Another problem is the unavailability of either the audio/video or computer equipment needed. The package may be unusable if one component is not available. To avoid this problem, each component should stand alone and be usable without the others. Thus, the audio- or videocassettes can still provide useful learning even if the program can't be used and vice versa.

Programs can be used to control the presentation of audio- and videocassettes. A special interface allows a computer to control the sequencing (start/stop) of the audio or video programs. This is usually referred to as *"random access"* media (it can be done with slides as well). This makes the audio or video program interactive; the program specifies the branching. The program may also be used to generate questions, graphics, process responses, etc.

Videodisc

Videodisc is an inherently interactive medium. Each frame on a videodisc has a unique address (number) and can be individually displayed as a still frame. This is true even of still frames that make up a dynamic sequence. Each frame can contain text, photographic, audio, or digital information (i.e., programs). For this reason, videodisc has the potential to eventually replace all other media.

Programs must be written to control the presentation of information stored on videodisc. These programs are identical to any other instructional program except that the information to be accessed may be a text or photographic still frame or a video/audio sequence. For example, here is a typical sequence of commands that might be contained in a program to show a motion sequence, then ask a question and provide feedback:

```
AUDIO 1 ON              {use audio channel 1}
PLAY 6000–7000          {show motion sequence}
DISPLAY 15010           {show question frame}
INPUT                   {accept input}
IF INPUT = "YES" 15050  {feedback for yes answer}
IF INPUT = "NO" 15060   {feedback for no answer}
```

Designing and implementing a videodisc program is identical to developing any other instructional program except that the screen displays are either motion sequences or still frames stored on the videodisc instead of computer displays. All the guidelines outlined in this book apply to the design of videodisc programs. However, the design of videodisc programs is more complex than ordinary instructional software because of the many options possible (e.g., multiple audio channels, motion or still frames, slow/fast motion, graphic overlays, etc.). For further information on the design of videodisc, see the references in the Appendix.

Classroom instruction

Software can be integrated into classroom instruction in the form of a hands-on activity added to the class. This is a fairly common component of courses that involve learning how to use a computer system. However, a hands-on activity can be added to classes on any subject, whether it is accounting, service, or sales training. The activity should involve a simulation/game, diagnostic test, applications software, or an expert systems program. Exercises or case studies that students solve using the software are developed by the instructor.

For example, imagine that you are teaching a workshop on the basic principles of supervision. After each principle has been explained and demonstrated via video sequences, workshop participants can use a simulation game that presents scenarios and requires them to make decisions about the best supervisory action. Alternatively, they could be provided with case studies in print or video form and an expert system program that helps them identify the best supervisory actions for each case study.

Successful hands-on activities require a classroom equipped with sufficient computers (two students to a computer is satisfactory unless individual results are desired). In addition, a video projector or large screen monitor is necessary so that the instructor can demonstrate the use of the software before students try it.

As computers become increasing prevalent in schools and training centers, this type of hands-on activity as part of a class will become increasingly common. It adds a valuable practice or diagnostic testing component to existing classroom instruction.

Specifications

An important design step for multimedia packages is the development of a course specification document. Table 4.1 lists some of the major items that should be specified. Instructional strategies should describe what each component of the course is intended to achieve and how. The equipment specification should state explicitly exactly what computer hardware and media equipment is needed. The software specification describes the characteristics of the program(s) involved. Lesson specifications should outline the content of print, audio, or video components. They can incorporate the lesson synopsis information described in Chapter 3. Packaging specifications tell how all the components will be physically assembled and provided to the student/instructor. The evaluation specification states how each component of the course will be evaluated in terms of its effectiveness.

While the development of a course specification document is desirable for any instructional program, it is especially critical for multimedia packages because of the increased complexity. This document will be important for developers as well as users.

Table 4.1   *Course Specifications*

Instructional Strategies
Equipment
Software
Lesson
Packaging
Evaluation

Summary

At present, instructional software is often used in conjunction with other media such as print, audio- or videocassettes, videodisc, or classroom delivery. It is important that the software be properly integrated with other media.

Print represents the most common media associated with software, especially in the form of user documentation. Effective documentation should be divided into short modules, clearly distinguish explanation from action, and provide descriptions of all likely outcomes for any particular action.

Software can be added to books, audio- and videocassette programs or classroom instruction in the form of simulations/games, diagnostic tests, applications programs, or expert systems. They provide a practice or testing component.

Programs can be written to control audio- or videocassettes or videodisc. Videodisc is an inherently interactive medium and can provide a highly sophisticated form of instructional software.

5

SCREEN DESIGN

Screen design is one of the most evident aspects of creating instructional software. Even though there are lots of components to software, screens are what people see and are often the primary factor used to judge the quality of programs. For this reason, a lot of attention should be given to the design of displays.

Relative to the design of the printed page, the design of screens is much more complex. Actually, the design of printed pages is pretty complex, but it is usually done by specialists (i.e., graphic designers and typographers). The author of a book does not usually have anything to do with the layout of pages or printing. There is a tendency for authors of software to do the design of their own screens, but this function would be better left in the hands of professional screen designers.

It will be helpful to begin our discussion of screen design by comparing it to the design of printed pages. Some of the major differences are as follows:

- ☐ Unlike print, blank space on a screen doesn't cost anything. Only information (i.e., text, graphics) is stored.
- ☐ The screen is a dynamic display medium. Text can appear anywhere at any time.
- ☐ There are capabilities such as blinking, sound effects, and color which can be used as attentional devices.
- ☐ You can control the rate at which information is displayed.
- ☐ The quality of screen displays is usually inferior to print.
- ☐ Screen displays can be modified much faster than print (in a networked system).

The guidelines in this and subsequent chapters address these differences.

Do not crowd screens

Since it does not cost anything to have blank space on a screen, there is no reason to crowd a lot of information into a single screen. As a general rule, put no more than twelve to sixteen lines of text and one graphic per screen. Break text up into short paragraphs of three or four sentences each with a double space between them. If you use windows or viewports as recommended below, you should have no problem with screen crowding.

There are two exceptions to this rule: first, the design of complex control panels or layouts used for simulations and games; and second, forms that have multiple fields to be filled in.

Each screen should
present one idea.

Try not to present
too much information
on a single screen!

Trying to cram too much
information on a single
screen is a very common
mistake in designing
screens. This mistake
results in screens that
are very hard to read and
very unattractive. Since
blank space is free, there
is no good reason to do

This . . .   *. . . Not this*

Avoid the use of scrolling and overlays

Since information can appear any place on the screen at any time, you have to make deliberate decisions about when to create a new screen and where to locate information. Unless you specifically create separate pages, information will continue to scroll from the bottom of the screen to the top. While scrolling may seem like a good idea, it quickly becomes very frustrating to the user. People tend to lose information as it rolls off the screen. It also becomes difficult for users to locate themselves in the program. For these reasons, always divide your program into separate pages. You may want to use scrolling in windows and viewports.

A second aspect of being able to display anything anywhere is the phenomenon of overlays. You have the capability to erase some portion of the screen and display something new, leaving everything else the same. The problem with overlays is that people often do not notice the new information that has been added. It is better either to create a new screen or use a window to introduce the new information. Overlays can save authoring time but possibly at the expense of student understanding.

Use attentional devices sparingly

Blinking (flashing), reverse video, color, and sound effects are devices that can be used to draw attention to something important on the screen. However, the value of these devices wears off quickly if they are overused and they become annoying to the user. As a general rule, only use one of these devices per screen.

Some special cautions are associated with the use of color and sound. Do not spend a lot of time worrying about the choice of particular colors because the actual hue displayed will depend upon how the user's monitor is tuned. What comes out as red on one monitor could be blue on another. Instead, pay attention to the contrast produced. A sharp contrast between the foreground and background will have the desired effect on any monitor.

When you use sound effects, be aware that they may be disturbing to others in the vicinity of the terminal (unless headphones are used). For this reason, it is highly recommended that you provide an "off" option at the beginning of a program if you are using sound effects or speech output extensively. Of course, you will have to provide redundant cues that take the place of the turned off sound or speech.

Use windows/viewports to organize information

Because information is presented dynamically on a screen, it is important to help users organize it as much as possible. The best way to do this is to create windows or viewports for menus, questions,

---

WINDOWING CAPABILITIES

Almost all current machines are capable of windows and viewports. However, machines that have bit-mapped display screens (e.g., the Apple Macintosh) feature extensive windowing capabilities. These include pop-up or pull-down menus that only appear when selected. The user also has the capability to modify the size or location of a window as desired. Under these circumstances, the designer specifies the content of the window and the default shape/location on the screen.

response or feedback areas, main concepts, examples, etc. This makes it easier and faster for people to understand what they are reading/seeing.

It is important to be consistent in the location and function of windows. Do not present a question or directions in one part of a screen and then use the same part on a successive screen for a response or feedback area. While variety in screen design is important, create the variety within functions.

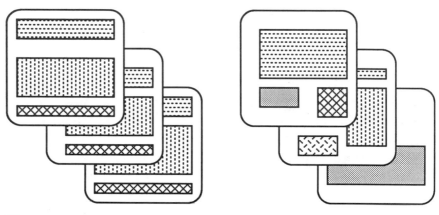

This . . .   *. . . Not this*

Use different type sizes and styles for emphasis and variety

Different sizes of type and different type styles (fonts) should be used for headings, labels, examples, questions, or any text that you want to stand out. This draws the attention of the user and makes the display more visually interesting.

Of course, it is possible to overdo this. On systems where a wide selection of type styles and sizes are available, be careful not to use too many combinations on any particular screen. As a general rule, there should be a maximum of four different type styles/sizes per display. It is also important to be consistent in the use of type styles and sizes, i.e., all major headings should be the same style and size, etc.

Use graphics whenever possible

Illustrations usually convey ideas much faster and are more easily remembered than words. For these reasons, graphics should be used as much as possible. Even subject matter that is inherently alpha-

The Whosiwhatsit

The Whosiwhatsit has
many complicated parts
which are very difficult
to explain in words such
as the thing which is
connected to the cludge
which is next to the

This . . .   *. . . Not this*

numeric (such as accounting, foreign languages, law) can be presented more effectively using graphics. This includes illustrations, figures, diagrams, sketches, or any other visual depiction. Graphics are especially useful for showing relationships, causes, sequences, and complex concepts.

Note that graphics are not always self-explanatory. Use labels or captions to explain a graphic. When using icons, you will probably need to provide an explanation of what each icon means. Also note that a high degree of realism or detail in graphics is usually not necessary or even desirable. In most cases, a line drawing is more effective than a full sketch or photograph.

One aspect of graphics use that is open for debate is the extent to which graphics should only be used when needed or for decorative purposes. Some people argue that graphics should only be used when they serve some real explanatory value. Others feel that graphics should be used to add aesthetic appeal to screen displays. This is not

---

GRAPHICS CAPABILITIES

The type of graphics possible will depend upon the display capabilities of the computer. The two major types of graphic displays are character and bit-mapped. With character displays you create your graphics in terms of individual characters that represent pieces of lines, curves, or symbols. With bit-mapped displays, you can address every point (called "pixels") on the screen. Needless to say, you can draw much more detailed graphics with bit-mapped displays.

an idle argument since the creation of graphics take considerable time and skill. Each designer has to make his or her own decision about this point.

"*Animation*" is a special graphics capability of computers (also possible with video). Animation involves moving objects or characters on the screen. It should be used to convey sequence or cause and effect. It can also be used simply as an attentional device.

Use titles and headings on all screens

One of the commonly reported problems with software is that users get lost and lose track of where they are (or were) in the program. This is because there are no physical clues about location (such as looking at how many pages are left). To overcome this problem, it is necessary to put titles or headings on all screens so that users can easily identify their location. It may be sufficient to show the section or unit, or it may be desirable to number every screen:

~~~~~~~~~~~~~ INTRODUCTION ~~~~~~~~~~~~ 5/16

Screen numbering will only work with programs that are page oriented. However, headings can be used with any type of program.

Screen resolution determines display quality

A major factor in determining the quality of the display is the screen resolution, i.e., how many individual points, or pixels, on the screen can be addressed by the computer. The resolution of the display will determine how distinct text and graphics appear. Ordinary television sets have relatively poor resolution (about 240 × 360 addressable points), whereas most computer monitors have higher resolution (about 400 × 600 addressable points). For comparison, a printed page has approximately 2,000 × 2,000 addressable points.

As a designer, your challenge is to produce the most attractive displays possible given the degree of screen resolution available. If you follow the design guidelines outlined in this chapter, you will be able to develop good screen displays, regardless of the characteristics of the computer or monitor used.

Summary

Here are the points made in this chapter about screen design:

- [ ] Do not crowd screens.
- [ ] Avoid the use of scrolling and overlays.
- [ ] Use attentional devices sparingly.
- [ ] Use windows/viewports to organize information.
- [ ] Use different type sizes and styles for emphasis and variety.
- [ ] Use graphics whenever possible.
- [ ] Use titles and headings on all screens.
- [ ] Screen resolution determines display quality.

6

USER CONTROL

If there is a single design rule that dictates the success of most software, it is this: The user should always be in control of the program. Software that fails to allow this will not usually be accepted by users. This chapter describes how to design programs that allow maximum user control.

When you design a program, imagine that you are designing the control panel of a car, airplane, or nuclear reactor, i.e., something to be operated by someone. Your major concern should be what kind of controls to provide the user and how to lay out the control panel. If you do a good job, people will be able to learn effortlessly and perhaps enjoyably. In fact, one of the most important goals for every software designer is to achieve complete transparency. In a "transparent" program, users completely forget that they are interacting with a computer program and focus totally on the task. Simulations and games frequently achieve transparency. In fact, if you want to see examples of complete transparency, visit a video game arcade sometime.

Always let the user set the pace

One of the most common and serious mistakes made in the design of programs is to have the program set the pace for the user. For example, the rate at which words, sentences, or graphics are displayed may be paced, or the length of time a screen is displayed may be controlled by the program. Since everyone reads at a different speed, controlling the rate of display means that most people will be forced to read faster or more slowly than their natural rate. Furthermore, if they are distracted for a few seconds or minutes, they may miss information.

To avoid this problem, always allow users to set their own pace by selecting the next display or event. Having the user press any key to continue is a common method of doing this. Also, put text and graphics on the screen as quickly as possible. Create attention by other effects (e.g., different type styles or sizes, boxing, highlighting) rather than by pauses or display timing.

An exception to this rule is animation. In an animated sequence you will want to control the timing for a brief period. However, you should allow the users to start the animation sequence so they feel some degree of control. Other exceptions include programs where timed presentation is important, such as a speed reading program or certain events in a simulation/game.

In some strategies, such as simulation and games, you may want to provide the user with a pause option. This allows the user to stop the action at any time and study the situation. Action is resumed when the pause is turned off.

Allow users to control sequencing

In addition to control of pacing, the user should also control all aspects of sequencing. This includes both intra and inter lesson sequencing. Within a lesson, the user should have the capability to go back to a previous screen, question, or event (i.e., undo) to get help or advice, and to exit at any time to a menu or command level. The review capability is needed because people often want to check what they just saw or did. (Starting over again from the beginning of a unit is not an acceptable form of backup!) The need for help at any time should be obvious. The capability to quit at any time allows people to interrupt the unit when they need to do something else.

Users should also be able to get to any lesson or part of the program from a main menu or command level. This means that users can decide in which order they would like to take lessons. Users should be able to go back through a lesson or sequence they have already completed and should not be locked out of any lesson.

A "resume" or "continue" option should be provided for when users exit from a unit to go look at something else and then want to return to the previous unit. This is especially important when a lot of work has been done in the unit which would take much trouble to repeat. This option should also be available each time users sign on to a previously started lesson. Expecting users to remember where they left off is not good enough! The resume option is particularly handy after an accidental sign-off (e.g., when somebody trips over the power plug).

Since instructional programs are often arranged in a carefully defined sequence according to prerequisites or objectives, allowing the capability to select any lesson in any order often upsets curriculum designers. (Of course, the situation is no different than a textbook or video where the user can decide what order they want to look at things.) To compensate for this, a check can be made at the beginning of each lesson to see if the user has completed the prerequisite lessons. If not, a message can be displayed which advises the user to complete the prerequisite lessons before continuing with the present lesson. However, the user should be allowed to continue and take the lesson if they want.

An exception to complete user control is the case of pre- and post-tests, exams, or questionnaires used to assess skill or knowledge level. Since this information is needed by the program (or is used for grades or certification), it must be taken at a certain place in the program (e.g., right after sign-on) and must be completed in full. However, the user should still have the capability to back up and skip questions, as well as change answers.

Use menus as much as possible

There are basically three ways to allow users to control a program (other than direct answers to questions): menus, command languages, and function keys. Menus consist of a list of options or selections. With a command language, special keywords or phrases are typed in. Function keys are additional keys provided on the keyboard that are assigned unique functions (e.g., help, next, exit) by the programmer. Function keys are usually labeled F1,F2,F3, etc.

Menus are better than command languages for instructional programs because they are quicker to learn, don't require memorizing keywords or parameters, and eliminate the possibility of syntax errors. Experienced users of a program usually prefer command languages, but almost everyone who uses an instructional program is new to the program and is only likely to use it once (or infrequently). Thus, the standard argument in favor of commands instead of menus does not really apply to instructional software.

Menus are used for two different purposes: to present control options and to present choices among content selections. Any time there are three or more options or choices, some form of menu is warranted. Menus can come in a variety of formats. Content selections are typically full-page menus that use a complete screen to list the alternatives. Control option menus usually consist of a list of options (words or icons) that are displayed along the top, bottom, or side of the screen. Bit-mapped display screens allow pop-up menus that appear in overlapping windows on the display once a keyword or icon is selected.

Function keys can be used in conjunction with menus by displaying the current function of each key along the bottom or side of the screen. This reminds the user what each function key does. It also provides a way to show when certain function keys are active/inactive or to redefine the function of a specific key in a program. In programs with some form of touch, trackball, or mouse input, icons can be used for the same purpose with a greater range of choices.

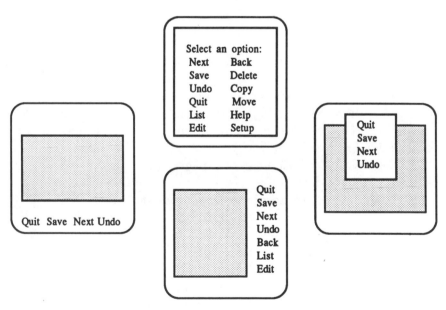

Menus can be at the top, bottom, side, full screen, or overlaid (pop-up).

Let the user customize the program

Almost every program has some aspect that users could change to suit their own needs, interests, or preferences. This includes characteristics of the display (e.g., window sizes, number of lines/columns per screen), the difficulty level of the presentation, or the actual content presented. The more customization capability provided, the more useful the program will be to the user.

The most important kind of customization is the ability to replace the content of the program in terms of examples, questions/problems, and feedback messages. One of the typical problems with any form of self-study instruction is that it can't be tailored to meet local needs or can't be updated easily. This problem is usually handled by only using the parts that are relevant or up-to-date. However, if you provide the capability for users to type in their own content easily, or modify content already there, this problem can be overcome. For example, in a spelling, foreign language, or mathematics lesson, you could allow the instructor (or student) to add new vocabulary, expressions, or problems. In a sales or management training program, new case studies or examples could be added. In a maintenance simulation, new faults or troubleshooting techniques could be added.

The ability to change difficulty levels is also a useful customization feature, especially for a program that will be used by people with a variety of backgrounds and skill levels. However, to have this kind of customization, it is necessary to create materials at different levels or to categorize the material created into different levels of difficulty. Generally, there will be three levels: the "normal" level of explanation appropriate for most users (medium difficulty), a more detailed explanation for those who lack the background (easy difficulty), and a "fast track" with a concise level of explanation (expert level). The major problem with difficulty levels is trying to identify good criteria to differentiate the categories for development and users.

The least useful kind of customization is the capability to allow users to input their own titles or data to be used in examples or problems. While this does add a personal touch, it is relatively trivial and does not impress users very much. Probably the worst form of such customization is insertion of the user's name in a fixed text sequence, e.g., "You did very well in the last lesson, John Smith." While this "form letter" technique may be valuable in programs for young children, it is annoying to most users over twelve years old. People feel they are being tricked by a phony gimmick . . . which they are.

Always provide defaults

To make it easier and faster for users to respond, every option should have a default action. If the user does not make a new choice (i.e., simply presses the RETURN/ENTER key or clicks the mouse), the default action will be taken. Default actions should always be displayed so that the user knows what the default is. The default action should be the most common or the safest choice for a response, the current file, or the last selection made. For example:

DO YOU WISH TO SAVE BEFORE EXITING? **YES** NO
NAME OF FILE TO SAVE: **LESSON1**
TRANSMISSION SPEED: 300 **1200** 2400

One of the major advantages of defaults for new or casual users is that they can select the defaults without having to know what the other options mean initially.

In selections where the choices are arbitrary, make the first option the default.

Provide multiple (redundant) control options

One of the difficulties in designing things for people is that they all have different preferences. The way to handle this with respect to program control is to provide multiple options that do the same thing. For example, options can be selected by moving the cursor or by a control key combination. If you wanted to quit, you could select the QUIT option on the menu or just press CONTROL Q. Alternatively, you could use function keys and menu options for the same functions or command words and menu options.

When you design redundant control options, you should focus on the difference between novice and experienced computer users. Novice users will generally prefer menus, while more experienced users will prefer control keys, function keys, and commands. Function keys are appropriate when you only need a small number of options (up to ten). Control keys can be used to represent a large number of options (up to about forty). Commands are typically used when the options have parameters (e.g., SPEED 1200) or can be combined.

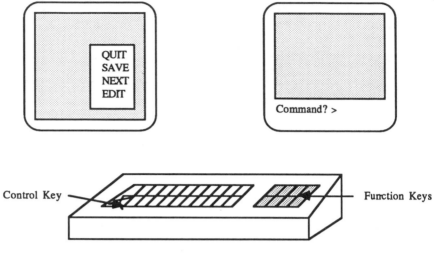

User control can be provided via menus, commands, control keys, and function keys.

By the way, another good reason for redundant control options is to allow the program to continue to function in the event of an equipment problem. For example, if you have written a program that is totally dependent on a mouse or trackball for selecting options and this device breaks, the user is out of luck. However, if you have provided a redundant set of control options via control or function keys, the program can still be used. Most systems that use touch input provide an alternative input mode through the keyboard in case the touch input is disabled or loses its calibration. The same precaution is taken with systems that use speech input.

Summary

Here are the guidelines for designing user control:

☐ Always let the user set the pace.
☐ Allow users to control sequencing.
☐ Use menus as much as possible.
☐ Let the user customize the program.
☐ Always provide defaults.
☐ Provide multiple (redundant) control options.

7

Response Analysis

This chapter presents guidelines for giving directions, asking questions, checking input, and providing feedback. All of these activities are related to the analysis of user responses. The way that directions or questions are phrased can make a big difference in the kind of responses made. Input checking is the heart of response analysis. Feedback tells users what happened to their response. As mentioned in Chapter 2, the kind of response analysis in a program determines the nature of the interactivity.

Figure 7.1 shows the major steps in response processing covered in this chapter. These steps will be required in any type of program and with any type of input.

State directions and questions so that errors are unlikely

A lot of input checking effort (and user frustration) can be eliminated by careful wording of directions and questions. Directions and questions should be phrased so that the expected answer is clear-cut. Say exactly what you want the user to do. Wherever possible provide an example as part of the directions or question. For example, consider the following input requests:

Enter the date:
What is the customer's name?
Do you know why Washington chopped down the cherry tree?

Each of these requests is ambiguous and is likely to lead to a variety of unexpected responses. Here are improved versions of these questions:

Type the date (mm/dd/yr):
Type the customer's name (first/last):

Figure 7.1

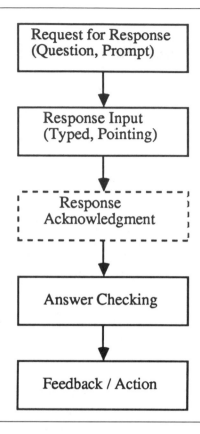

Type a sentence that explains why Washington chopped down the cherry tree:

Notice the nature of the changes to the questions. First, they state exactly what the user is expected to do (i.e., type something). Secondly, they described the expected format for the answer. However, even these improvements still contain quite a lot of ambiguity. For example, do you have to enter two numbers for month/day or will one do? Do you put slashes between the numbers or names? Should the sentence have punctuation? Here are better versions of the three questions:

Type the date (e.g., 02/25/88):
Type the customer's name (e.g., John Smith):

Type a sentence that explains why Washington chopped down the cherry tree (punctuation not needed).

Making your directions or questions as clear as possible will not totally eliminate all potential mistakes or confusion, but it will sure help! If you find it very difficult to state the directions clearly, it may be a hint that the program (or the specific response required) is too complicated.

Use pointing rather than typed input whenever possible

Design menus and questions so that the user selects an option via some form of pointing response (arrow keys, mouse, touch, etc.) rather than by typing something from the keyboard. This eliminates the need for error checking and allows the user to respond faster. Any type of computer can be programmed for some type of pointing response. For example, the space bar can be used to move across the options and the ENTER/RETURN key pressed to select something.

Clearly, questions that require text or numerical input or that involve a recall rather than recognition type answer will require the use of the keyboard. Actually, it is possible to do this by pointing too, since numbers or letters can be displayed on the screen and selected one at a time. Most arcade games (which lack keyboards) use this method for entry of names or numerical information.

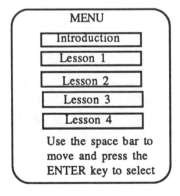

MENU

Introduction
Lesson 1
Lesson 2
Lesson 3
Lesson 4

Use the space bar to move and press the ENTER key to select

MENU
----
1. Introduction
2. Lesson 1
3. Lesson 2
4. Lesson 3
5. Lesson 4

Type the number of the option you want:

This . . .   *. . . Not this*

Always acknowledge user input

Programs should provide a response for every user input even if it is just an acknowledgment such as "ok" or "wait". Users need to know that their input has been recognized by the program. Normally, a response will result in an immediate feedback message or change in the display. When the response may take more than a few seconds (e.g., complex calculations in a simulation or a search in a large database), a "wait" message should be displayed from the time the input is made until the response is provided.

Exceptions to the need for acknowledgment are displays involving multiple fields. Advancing to the next field is usually sufficient acknowledgment of input.

Answer analysis should be tolerant of variations in response

With typed input, it is necessary to check for variations in responses provided. For example, your program should ignore the case (i.e., upper/lower) of the response unless this is relevant to the answer. Blank spaces before or after the answer should not matter either. It's also a good idea to check for common keyboard confusions such as typing O for 0 (i.e., the letter O for zero) or l for 1 (i.e., the letter l for one) and vice versa.

Many authoring programs allow you to set a spelling tolerance for answer matching. If the answer contains only one or two incorrect letters, the response is judged as an acceptable match. In addition, you can usually specify exactly what part of an answer is important and must be in the response using some type of delimiter. The parts of the answer that are irrelevant can be indicated by using "wild card" characters.

For example, suppose that you were interested in matching the specific phrase "computers are wonderful". You would specify this in the following form: %c*mput*rs*are*w*nderful*%, where the percent signs specify the exact string to be matched, and the asterisks denote positions in the answer where any character is acceptable ("wild cards"). The following answers would be acceptable matches according to this specification:

> computors are wonderfull
> cumputers are wunderful
> computersare wonderful

The following phrases, however, would not match this specification:

computer are wonderful
computers are wonderous
computers are not wonderful

Of course, the answer specification could be changed to allow a wider range of alternatives if desired. This is up to the author.

One of the major frontiers in the design of user interfaces is natural language and speech input. Most people would prefer to interact with a computer by typing or speaking in regular English (or whatever language) sentences and phrases. Clearly this would allow programs to be much more tolerant of variations in user responses. On the other hand, a tremendous amount of knowledge is required by the program to understand what the user means. This knowledge must be provided by the author and involves a great deal of work, far beyond the current levels of effort associated with developing instructional software. Research in the areas of artificial intelligence and expert systems is concerned with how to design and develop such natural language and speech recognition capabilities (see references in Appendix).

NATURAL LANGUAGE AND SPEECH RECOGNITION CAPABILITIES

Natural language understanding and speech recognition capability are now widely available and in use with many types of programs and machines (including personal computers). However, these capabilities are still fairly limited in terms of the size of the vocabulary they can handle (typically only a few hundred words). With speech recognition, there is the additional problem of accents and idiosyncratic pronunciation. Current capabilities are acceptable for a number of applications; however, further advances in the field of artificial intelligence are needed for this to be a routine feature of programs.

Allow users to change their answers

One thing to keep in mind when designing response processing sequences is that people frequently make inadvertent choices or change their mind about answers they have made. For this reason, users should be able to change their answers or selections before they are processed. This is especially true of responses that have important consequences, such as:

- ☐ deleting a file, function, or data records
- ☐ saving something with a name that already exists (i.e., replacement)
- ☐ exiting from a program without saving current work
- ☐ any data entered that will be used often in the program (e.g., names, dates, times, addresses)

Before one of these actions is processed by the program, the user should be asked for a confirmation:

> Are you sure you want to delete the file _____ ? OK CANCEL
> The mailing address is _____ CORRECT INCORRECT

The general technique is to redisplay the specific action requested or data entered and ask if this is correct. If users indicate that it is not correct, they are returned to the previous menu or the question so that they can correct the response or do something else.

Responses should always require a separate keypress (i.e., the ENTER/RETURN key) to allow users to make corrections before the response is processed. With typed input, users can employ the backspace key to change their answer before pressing ENTER/RETURN. With a pointing response, they can select another option before entering. Response analysis in which the answer is processed as soon as a certain number of characters are typed, or as soon as an option is selected, does not give users a chance to change their mind or correct errors and is poorly designed.

The ability to change answers is particularly important in tests and quizzes. In a paper and pencil test, students have the capability to review questions and change their answers if they want. It is important to provide the same capability in a computer based test. This means that students should be able to go back and look at previous questions, see the answers they picked and change the answers. This capability should be available at any time during the test, not just at the end.

In terms of program design, this review and "rub-out" capability means that your program will need to have BACK and NEXT options to allow students to get to the question they want to review, and you will need to display their current answer. If the questions are randomly selected or generated, you will need to store them so they can be redisplayed.

When the student goes back to a question that was previously answered, the cursor should be located on the last character of a typed answer (so he or she can backspace to erase it) or on the previously selected option in a pointing type response. If the student decides not to change the previous answer, the current response or option selected stays the same when ENTER/RETURN is pressed.

Always provide corrective feedback for errors or wrong answers

When the user makes an error or types an incorrect answer to a question, the feedback message should suggest the correct format for the answer. Avoid messages that tell users they made an "error"or that they were "wrong." For example:

Type in the date (mm/dd/yr): **31/5/86**
ERROR 069: First field exceeds acceptable range

Not only is this type of error message intimidating, it is also not very helpful in explaining what the error is. A better error message would be:

The number you have entered for the month is too large.
Type the month first, then the day and year.

This error message makes it clear what the problem is and doesn't affront the user. An even better error message would be:

Do you mean 5/31/86? YES NO

This message allows the user to make the correction without having to retype the date. In order to have this type of error message, it is necessary to know (or guess) what kinds of errors are likely to be made.

Feedback should be brief and neutral in tone

Feedback messages should be brief (e.g., single words whenever possible). When the response is incorrect or inappropriate, a brief explanation should be provided (or the user should be directed toward HELP for a full explanation).

Many designers feel that it is important to provide variety in feedback messages. Instead of using the same "Correct" or "OK" message for each answer, they prefer to randomly generate a different message each time (e.g., "Right," "Good," "That's it," etc.) from a stored list. There is no evidence to suggest that this is very important to students.

Sarcasm or any sort of demanding feedback messages should be avoided. It is not pleasant to receive messages such as:

> You sure messed up that question! Let's try again.
> That was a pretty poor answer. How about another try.
> Stupid! We just learned that. I'll give you one more chance.

Humor in feedback messages should be avoided in most circumstances. The problem with using humor is that its effectiveness varies tremendously across individuals. What some people find funny, others will find offensive or puzzling. Unless you are sure that the humor will work for all users, you should skip it.

Summary

Here are the guidelines for response analysis presented in this chapter:

- ☐ State directions and questions so that errors are unlikely.
- ☐ Use pointing rather than typed input whenever possible.
- ☐ Always acknowledge user input.
- ☐ Answer analysis should be tolerant of variations in response.
- ☐ Allow users to change their answers.
- ☐ Always provide corrective feedback for errors or wrong answers.
- ☐ Feedback should be brief and neutral in tone.

8

Helps

Helps represent one of the more powerful and unobtrusive forms of interactive instruction. They are powerful because they can provide very specific information exactly when it is needed. They are unobtrusive because the information is hidden until the user requests it.

Helps are a form of embedded training, i.e., instruction that is an integral part of a computer-based system or product. Embedded training can be built into any type of automated office or manufacturing system, computer-controlled equipment (such as aircraft, appliances, "smart" weapons, etc.), and any type of computer system (e.g., administrative, banking, inventory, retail sales). As more and more systems and products become computer-based, embedded training will become increasingly common.

There are a number of different types of helps. "Fixed format" (or context independent) helps produce the same information regardless of what the user has done. The most familiar kind of fixed format help is an explanation of a command. Online reference manuals or job aids are also common examples of fixed format helps. Fixed format helps are the simplest type of help to implement since they involve the creation of text files.

In contrast, "context-sensitive" helps provide information that depends upon what the user is currently trying to do. For example, if you were in the middle of a spreadsheet creating a formula and you asked for help, you would get information about creating formulas. Later, if you were editing the same formula and you asked for help, you would get information about editing formulas. With a context-sensitive help, the program attempts to provide information specific to your current activity.

"Prompting" type helps are similar to context-sensitive helps except that they are generated by the system rather than being requested by the user. For example, if a user types a command in the wrong format or with the wrong parameters, a prompting help system will automatically display the correct format of the command. A sophisticated help system will actually attempt to correct the mistake and display the corrected command to the user for verification (i.e., "Did you mean . . .").

"Query-in-depth" helps provide multiple levels of information. Each successive help request provides more elaboration or detail than the previous level. Thus, if you ask for an explanation of a particular command, the first help may simply provide the purpose and correct format. A second request for help may provide examples of use or a full description of how and when the command can be used. A third request may produce the full documentation on the command from the reference manual. These different levels of help may be accessed by successive help requests or the level may be set as a parameter of the program. A common way of implementing query-in-depth is to put increasingly more detailed information in successive help screens and allow the user to return to the application after each help screen or continue with more helps.

"Dialog" type helps allow the user to ask questions in a conversational format. Such helps depend upon some form of natural language understanding capability to work. Users type their question in natural language. The following is an example of a dialog type help sequence.

USER: How do I copy all my files to a new diskette?

HELP: Use the command, copy a:*.*b:

USER: What are a: and b:?

HELP: a: refers to the left drive and b: refers to the right drive

USER: I still don't understand what to do.

HELP: To make a complete copy of a diskette, put the source diskette in the left drive and the new diskette in the right drive, then type the command, copy a:*.*b: and press ENTER.

USER: OK, thanks.

HELP: You're welcome.

Needless to say, there are only a few systems available today capable of this advanced type of help (see the article by Wilensky et al. about the UNIX Consultant in the Appendix).

The last type of help to be mentioned is "adaptive" helps. An adaptive help keeps track of how much the user knows about the system and adjusts the level of help information provided accordingly. Thus, a request for help at a particular place will produce different information when the user is new than when the user is more familiar with the system. Alternatively, the help system may limit the actual functions available to the user until certain basic operations have been mastered. To have an adaptive help capability, it is usually necessary for the program to build a user model that represents what the user currently knows about the system. This model is used to make decisions about what kind of help to present to the user. Adaptive helps are very similar to intelligent tutoring systems (see references in Appendix).

Make helps as specific as possible

In order to be helpful, helps must provide the specific information needed by the user. Table 8.1 lists some of the typical categories of information that users may need help with. To be comprehensive, a help system would provide this kind of information for every function and operation in a program.

In a fixed format type of help, there should be a help associated with every command or option. In a context-sensitive help system, there should be a help associated with every response sequence. One way of identifying all possible helps needed is to construct a matrix with functions or operations down the side and sequences or units across the top (see Figure 8.2). Each cell in the matrix is a potential help.

Table 8.1   *Categories of Helps That May Be Needed*

1. Information about current location or status
2. Description of current options
3. Explanation of what things do (e.g., commands)
4. Description of format for input
5. Explanation of error messages/conditions
6. Explanation of output displays
7. Information about how the program works
8. Explanation of terms (glossary)

Figure 8.2

	Unit1	Unit2	Unit3	Unit4	Unit5
Add	X			X	
Copy			X		X
Delete	X				X
Rename			X	X	
Replace		X	X		X
Exit	X			X	X

Different types of helps are needed for different users

Because of differences in background experiences and interests, different types of helps will be needed for different types of users. One dimension of difference is computer experience. Users who have little experience with computers will need help with very basic things, such as being reminded to press the ENTER/RETURN key after selecting a response or putting diskettes in a disk drive correctly. On the other hand, experienced computer users will need more sophisticated help having to do with shortcuts and limitations. One of the ironies about these two groups of users is that they are both likely to be very impatient and intolerant of the computer — but for quite different reasons. The novice doesn't want to learn any more than necessary to use the machine; the expert wants to learn how to do things as quickly and efficiently as possible.

Research shows that inexperienced computer users are often overwhelmed and confused by help systems. This suggests that help systems intended for novices should be either fairly simple (i.e., fixed format) or very sophisticated (i.e., prompting or dialog). Help systems designed for novices should not add more complexity to the use of the system!

Users also differ in terms of their reasons for using a computer. Some people will need to use a computer system infrequently (e.g., to perform annual inventories, generate monthly reports, or update customer records). Other people will use a computer system on a routine basis for most of their work (e.g., bank tellers, reservation clerks, travel agents). Casual users will likely need different types of helps than frequent users.

The best way to determine what types of helps are needed by different groups of users is to observe their use of the system and identify the problems they have. Listings of their online sessions can be analyzed to identify the kinds of errors made and helps can be developed for these errors. Once the helps are implemented, the analysis process is repeated to see how well the helps work and what new problems arise. Note that this is a general methodology for designing helps; it is not just for discovering the differences between different user groups.

Incidentally, a major problem with identifying helps for different types of users is that users tend to change categories. A novice computer user can quickly become an experienced user after using the system a few times. Casual users may become frequent users and vice versa. It is a good idea to allow users to set the kind or level of help provided so they can tailor it to their current level and needs. This can be done by providing a menu that allows the user to set the help options (or turn help off completely if desired).

The default setting for the help options should be full explanations rather than no helps. The program instructions should tell the user about the ability to change the help options. If there is a help for help, it should also explain how to change help levels.

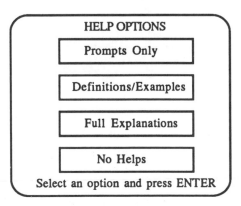

Allow users to specify the level of help.

Helps should always be available and easy to access

It seems relatively obvious that if helps are to be useful they must be available whenever needed and they must be easy to get to. However, helps are frequently not provided for all functions/operations in a program and they are sometimes "hidden" from the user. It is critical that helps be complete and easy to access.

If helps are only available at certain times or places in a program, there should be some kind of indication of when help is available. This is usually done by displaying the word "help" or a help icon somewhere on the screen when help is active.

Helps can be activated via a fixed or function key, a typed command, or selection of an option that is always displayed on the screen. On some keyboards, there is a key labeled "Help". It is common to use the F1 function key for help. The standard typed command for help is the word "help"or a question mark. Usually, it is also possible to type specific help commands such as "help print" or "? save". With keys or typed commands, it is necessary to remind the user that help is available. With a continuously displayed help option, the user is always aware of its availability.

It is important to design helps so that they do not disrupt the work flow of the user. Helps must always return the user to the point in the program where they left off to get help. It is highly desirable to provide help information in a window that overlays the current application. When the user is finished with the help, the window should disappear. If a window can't be used and new displays are required for the help, the original application display should be recreated when the user returns from the help. Helps that cause the original application to scroll off the screen make it difficult for users to remember where they left off (and sometimes what their exact problem was).

Ensure that help information is accurate and complete

The information provided by helps must be correct and complete otherwise the user's trust and confidence in the system will be undermined. If the helps explain that a function works one way and the user finds that it actually works differently, the user is not likely to believe any other help information provided (even if it is accurate). Quality review methods (see Chapter 9) are especially important for helps.

A common reason helps are inaccurate or contain omissions is because changes have been made to the system or product but the helps have not been updated. To prevent this problem, it is critical to establish development procedures that require help information to be changed at the same time as the application functions. This is accomplished most easily if the help functions are considered to be a major part of the application and hence have the same revision priority as any other part of the system.

One important kind of information often missing from helps is examples. Examples provide concrete illustrations and are sometimes the easiest type of help information to understand. Examples should cover typical situations as well as counter-examples and anomalies. For example:

```
>help print
.The PRINT command prints out all or part of a document or file.
.It has the format PRINT [Starting page] [Ending page]
.Examples:
    PRINT 1,20    prints pages 1 to 20 inclusive
    PRINT 10      prints page 10
    PRINT 10,     prints all pages starting with page 10
    PRINT ,20     prints pages 1 to 20 inclusive (same as    PRINT 1,20)
    PRINT         prints all pages
    PRINT -1,20   prints pages 1 to 20 inclusive
.Note that negative numbers and zero are treated as 1
```

In a context-sensitive type of help system, it is possible to tailor the examples to the user's current situation. For example, if the user is currently using a certain file, the help may insert this file name in the examples used.

The help information provided to the user is sometimes incomplete because the user did not request all of the information available. For example, a user might set the help level to definitions only, but the information needed for a specific problem might only be provided in the full explanation mode. This problem can be minimized if the description of the help system (i.e., help help) explains what kind of information is provided by different levels of help or different types of help requests. It is also a good idea to provide an index and cross-reference for helps accessed from a help submenu. In addition, helps that only provide partial information should indicate that further information is available and how to access it (e.g., "Press help again to see examples or ENTER to continue with the program").

Summary

Here are the guidelines presented in this chapter for the design of helps:

- ☐ Make helps as specific as possible.
- ☐ Different types of helps are needed for different users.
- ☐ Helps should always be available and easy to access.
- ☐ Ensure that help information is accurate and complete.

9

Error Handling

We live in a world of imperfection. Everybody makes misstakes. This realization applies to the development of instructional software in two ways: finding the errors in your program and dealing with errors made by students when using the program. This chapter discusses both types of error handling.

A number of factors will affect the likelihood of errors in programs. If an authoring system (see Chapter 1) is used to create the program, the program should be free of bugs. If user responses are always made via menus (as recommended in Chapter 6), the kinds of errors possible are reduced considerably. If directions and questions are stated clearly (as discussed in Chapter 7), the chances of an incorrect response being made are less.

The way a program is designed and implemented can also affect the likelihood of errors. Programs should be designed, developed, and tested in small pieces, or "modules." Errors in a program are

---

BENEFITS OF MODULARIZATION

Modularization (dividing a lesson or program into small units) is an important design concept. Not only does it make it easier to debug a program but it also makes it easier to revise a program. Only the modules that need revisions are changed; other modules can be left alone. In addition, modularization increases user control since it allows the user to get in and out of the program easier (assuming the modules are accessible). Try to divide your program into modules that are no longer than 15 to 20 minutes each.

much easier to find and fix if modules are created and tested individually and then combined.

Test your program for both expected and unexpected responses

There are basically two kinds of student answers you need to check for: expected responses and unexpected responses. Expected responses are the answers that students would make if they were responding as you anticipated. This includes correct and incorrect answers to questions or problems and selection of options in a menu. Unexpected responses are responses that students shouldn't make. This includes pressing special keys (e.g., ESCAPE, back space, tab) or unusual combinations of keys, entering text when numbers should be entered (or vice versa), pointing to things outside of the response area (e.g., the screen border), and incorrect punctuation.

Keep in mind that most of these unexpected responses are accidental, not deliberate. This is why they are usually nonsensical and difficult to anticipate. For example, a user meant to press the shift key to type a capital "C" but instead pressed the control key and entered control "C". In many programs, control "C" is a command used to interrupt processing. Suppose that a user presses the F1 key (a function key) when they meant to just press the "1" key. If the function keys are used for user control options, the response will be different than expected. In many cases, overanxious users press the ENTER/RETURN key before they have typed their response. This results in a blank response.

To properly test your program for errors, you need to try every possible input response for every possible input sequence. This exhaustive testing of all possibilities is called "bullet-proofing." A program that has been completely bullet-proofed can handle any response, no matter how bizarre (including turning off the machine). The program should respond to an unexpected answer by restating the desired response or option(s).

Bullet-proofing is not as difficult as it may sound, although it can be very tedious and time-consuming. Most input sequences can be programmed so that any response other than the expected ones are directed to the same error message. Once this error handling routine has been thoroughly checked, it can be used throughout the program with the knowledge that it will work for every input sequence it is included in. Bullet-proofing then reduces to checking that the routine has been correctly placed in every input sequence.

Bullet-proofing typed input is much more difficult than bullet-proofing menu selections. You have to worry about punctuation, upper/lower case, word order, blank spaces, incorrect symbols (e.g., $+ \setminus = / - \&$"), not to mention the content of the answer. Even something as simple as a numerical answer can lead to problems with commas and decimal places (e.g., 1000.0 versus 1,000).

The real dilemma with bullet-proofing is that there is no way to know for sure that your program will catch all errors. Until the day when somebody discovers a reliable technique for providing the correctness of a program, it is all a matter of trial and error. The more trials, the fewer errors.

INDEPENDENT TESTING

For a number of reasons, it is highly desirable to have an independent group test your software. It ensures that the testing gets done thoroughly and eliminates a tedious development step for you. There are a number of companies and organizations that will test and certify your software (e.g., the International Bureau of Software Testing in Massachusetts).

Check the range of answers

One simple but highly useful error handling technique is range checking. This means checking the user's response to see if it is within an acceptable range for the answer. In the case of a numerical response, the number entered could be too small or too large. For example, if you asked the user to enter the heart rate in a medical simulation, the correct range would be from 0 to 200. Any number outside of that range would produce a message such as "The number you entered is too high (low), please re-enter."

With text answers, the appropriate range to check is the number of characters or words anticipated. Thus if the correct answer is a ten-letter word or a phrase consisting of three words, any answer that has more than ten letters or three words is incorrect. Note that a few extra characters or words should be allowed for since the user may add space or articles (i.e., the, a).

Draw the user's attention to an error

Error messages are often not noticed by users because the error message doesn't attract their attention. For example, an error message may be displayed at the bottom or top of the screen and then disappear when any key is pressed. The user may press a key before ever seeing the message. The worst kind of error messages are those that simply flash on the screen for a few seconds and are then erased. If users look away during this instant (perhaps to look something up in a manual), they never see the message.

Error messages should catch the user's attention by being displayed in a separate window and require the user to make some sort of response. For example, an attempt to load or delete a file that doesn't exist should produce a message like:

File do.dat does not exist. Press ENTER to repeat the command.

Error messages that are fairly serious in nature should be accompanied by a tone. For example, an attempt to save a file that already exists or a disk full error should provoke an auditory warning.

ifhkshfjshfkjhfskfhkjhhfkj
sfjlksfjskfkhsfjsldjskjfklsj
slsifskislfskfjskskisksisiff
sdf　　　　　　　　　　ll
sds　　ERROR!　　
fjsk　　　　　　　　　　j
ssjhsjhjshjsfssjhsjfsjsfsdjs
jsjhfsjfhsjfhsjhsdjhfjhfsjhf
sfjskfjsdfjsdkjfskfjskfjkjfk
xnvslfslfjskjkofwsfjsslfjsf

ifhkshfjshfkjhfskfhkjhhfkj
sfjlksfjskfkhsfjsldjskjfklsj
slsjfskjslfskfjskskjsksjsjff
sdfhjfsfsfjsjflsfdjsfjslljlafll
sdsadsdrrrf error fnskfjfej
fjskfskfshsjkhsjhsjhsjhsfj
ssjhsjhjshjsfssjhsjfsjsfsdjs
jsjhfsjfhsjfhsjhsdjhfjhfsjhf
sfjskfjsdfjsdkjfskfjskfjkjfk
xnvslfslfjskjkofwsfjsslfjsf

This . . .

. . . Not this

Tell the user how to correct the problem

There is nothing more frustrating to a user than to receive an error message and have no idea what to do next. An error message should clearly state the nature of the problem (in English, not Computerese) and how to recover from the error. For example:

DISK DRIVE NOT READY   ABORT,IGNORE,RETRY?>

is a common error message received on a personal computer when you type a command that involves reading a diskette. What does this message mean and what are the recovery options? Typically, this error message means that the latch on the disk drive is not closed. The recovery options are cancel (ABORT), continue (IGNORE), or repeat (RETRY) the command. A clearer version of this message would be:

Close the latch on the disk drive door. CANCEL CONTINUE REPEAT

In some cases, there may be no recovery action possible for an error. One of the most notorious such errors is when a user tries to save a file and there is no space left on the disk. With some programs and systems, it is not possible to insert another disk at this point and hence the save cannot be completed. This may mean that the user loses all work done in the current session. The error message should indicate that no recovery is possible. It is the responsibility of system designers to design programs so that this kind of "fatal" error does not occur under normal circumstances.

Always "fail soft" if possible

When an unexpected response causes the program to fail, the program should allow the user to continue, resume, or restart with minimal disruption and loss of work. Failing in a way that allows the user to recover is called "failing soft" as opposed to "failing hard," which leaves the user helpless. For example, consider the most insidious of all computer failures: you accidently pull out the plug, or the power fails. A good program will allow you to reconstruct what you were doing before the power went out.

Designing a program with good error recovery involves a lot of thought about what kinds of problems might arise and how to deal with them. It also involves keeping track of what the user is doing so that if something goes wrong, the last state can be reconstructed. The difficult part about designing error recovery procedures is that you do not know why, how, or where the program will fail (since it is likely to be caused by a bug you don't know about).

A powerful UNDO function that "undoes" the most recent action is probably the best single "fail soft" capability.

Summary

Here are the guidelines for error handling:

☐ Test your program for both expected and unexpected responses.
☐ Check the range of answers.
☐ Draw the user's attention to the error.
☐ Tell the user how to correct the problem.
☐ Always "fail soft" if possible.

10

Revision

An important phase of authoring takes place after the initial program has been developed. This is the process of revision as a result of quality review, pilot testing, or actual use. In fact, the quality of much instructional software comes from the changes made in the revision process, not the original version. It is essential to think of revision as a routine part of authoring activity, not something that is done just to "fix up" the program. Design is an iterative rather than linear process and involves continual changes.

When making revisions, you should be careful to base your changes on data and design guidelines rather than personal preferences. Everyone will have a slightly different opinion about how a screen should be organized or how a question should be phrased. Trying to keep everyone happy will drive you nuts! On the other hand, if different people make the same suggestions, then you should probably make the changes.

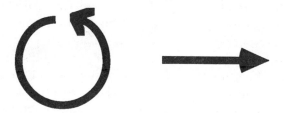

Design is an iterative, not linear, process.

Use a checklist to systematically review the quality of a program

An important step in developing high-quality software is a systematic review that checks each unit or sequence in the program for design flaws. A checklist is very helpful for this purpose. Table 10.1 provides an example of a quality review checklist. It covers the guidelines discussed in the previous chapters plus considerations for content and language.

Since the content and language considerations are new, a few words of explanation are in order. Content considerations include purpose, level, sequence, accuracy, and completeness. The instructional goal or objective of a program should be stated in an introduction (unless this is stated in ancillary materials). The sequencing of the program should take into account prerequisites among lessons. The level of the content should be appropriate for the students the program is designed for. The content should be accurate and complete.

Language considerations include reading level, bias, slang expressions, spelling, grammar, and punctuation. Reading level represents the major factor determining how easy or hard it is to comprehend the text of your program. One of the interesting findings about reading level is that a lower reading level is better for everybody. (Better readers just read faster.) In fact, text written at a fifth-grade reading level appears to be best for most users. A conversational style is generally recommended for all text.

There are many kinds of bias that can creep into language. This includes cultural, sexual, and racial bias. If you have ever used instructional materials developed by someone in another country, you will probably have noticed cultural bias — unfamiliar expressions, different forms of spelling, etc. Sexual bias refers to making assumptions about the sex of a person based upon role stereotypes (e.g., doctors are always male; nurses are always female) and the constant use of male referents (e.g., he, his, salesman). In a civilized society that is committed to sexual equality, this type of bias in language is unacceptable. The same remarks hold for any sort of racial bias.

The avoidance of any sort of jargon, slang, or idioms is important. The use of such terms or expressions introduces cultural bias and limits the number of people who will understand what is being said. Furthermore, it tends to date your program. So, be hip and cool it on the buzz words, you dig?

Finally, you need to check spelling, grammar, and punctuation. While these kinds of mistakes may seem like a small matter, they can be distracting to the user. They also give the impression of careless-

Table 10.1   *Quality Review Checklist*

1. Content
   • Is the purpose of the program stated?
   • Is the sequence appropriate?
   • Is the level correct?
   • Is the information accurate and complete?

2. Language
   • Is the reading level too high?
   • Is the language free of bias?
   • Is the language free of jargon, slang, and idioms?
   • Are the spelling, grammar, and punctuation correct?

3. Displays
   • Are the screens too crowded?
   • Are scrolling and overlays avoided?
   • Are windows used to organize information?
   • Are graphics used whenever possible?
   • Are different type styles/sizes used?
   • Are titles and headings used?

4. User Control
   • Do users control the pace?
   • Can users control the sequence?
   • Are menus used as much as possible?
   • Can users customize the program?
   • Are there multiple control options?
   • Are defaults provided?

5. Response Analysis
   • Are directions and questions stated clearly?
   • Is pointing input used wherever possible?
   • Is user input always acknowledged?
   • Does answer analysis tolerate response variation?
   • Can users change their answers easily?
   • Is corrective feedback provided?
   • Are feedback messages brief and neutral?

6. Helps
   • Are helps as specific as possible?
   • Are different levels of helps provided?
   • Are helps always available and easy to access?
   • Is help information accurate and complete?

ness or inaccuracy. This can undermine the credibility of the subject matter and the program.

Use student response data to find flaws in the instruction

One of the ways in which revision of instructional software differs from that of traditional materials is the availability of detailed response data. This was touched upon briefly in Chapter 3. Every time the student makes a response, the nature of the response can be recorded. The response data collected can be used to evaluate student performance and to evaluate the effectiveness of the instruction. It is the latter purpose that is of interest for revision.

A standard way of examining student response data is to look at a frequency table that shows the response of each student to every question, option, or input request of the program. Figure 10.2 shows an example of this kind of frequency table. Each row represents a different student and each column represents a unique question. The entries indicate different types of responses (1 for correct response, 0 for incorrect, ? for help request, and blank for skipped). The row totals indicate the number of correct responses the student got across all questions; the column totals indicate the number of times each

Figure 10.2

		Question Number						
		Q1	Q2	Q3	Q4	Q5	Q6	Total
Student		---	---	----	---	---	----	------
	S1	0	0	0	1	0		1
	S2	1	0	?	1	1	0	3
	S3	0	?	?	?	?	?	0
	S4	1	1	1				3
	S5	1	0	1	1	1	1	5
	S6	1		0	1	0	1	3
	S7	0	0	1	1	1	0	3
	S8	?	?	1	1	0	1	3
Total		4	1	4	6	3	3	21

question was answered correctly. Of course, it would be possible to total each type of response if desired (i.e., number of correct, incorrect, helps, or skipped).

The data provided by Figure 10.2 suggests some possible problems with the lesson. For example, only one student answered question 2 correctly. This suggests that there is a problem with the presentation of information the question is associated with, or that the question is poorly worded, or that the question is too difficult for most students. On the other hand, most of the students got question 4 correct. Perhaps it is too easy and should be dropped or revised.

Note that the table also gives us some insight into the behavior of certain students. Student 3 avoided answering all of the questions after the first one by using help. The lesson may have been too difficult (or boring) for this student. Student 4 answered the first three correctly and then skipped the rest. The lesson could have been too easy for this student.

It is important to realize that the data provided by the frequency table only suggests problems with the lesson. To find out if there really is a problem and its exact nature, it is necessary to make changes and collect more data. It is also important to interview students and find out why they responded as they did. In other words, this kind of data gives you ideas about potential problems with the instruction, but you then have to track down the specifics through further questioning.

The data table shown in Figure 10.2 is only one type of analysis that you can perform. Figure 10.3 shows another kind of data table that produces an item frequency matrix. This table tells you exactly what choices were made by each student for a particular question. The choices could be different response alternatives in a multiple-choice question, selections from a menu, or words/phrases matched by keywords. In the latter case, it is common to provide a list of all words typed in that were not matched. This helps determine what additional keywords should be added.

The column totals in Figure 10.3 indicate the number of times each alternative was selected. Note that student 3 picked two alternatives (A1, A5). This suggests that A5 was a help or hint that resulted in the selection of A1. In questions where the student can make a number of selections, it is often useful to show the order of selection in the table.

Figure 10.3

		A1	A2	A3	A4	A5
COURSE: ENG001			LESSON: FUND02			QUES: 013
			Response Alternatives			
Student		—	—	—	—	—
	S1	1				
	S2			1		
	S3	1				1
	S4		1			
	S5				1	
	S6				1	
Total		2	1	1	2	1

Instead of (or in addition to) responses, it is also possible to record the amount of time it took a student to respond to a question or to complete a module. The time taken to respond to a question (or choose an option) is called "response latency." It is measured from the time the question, problem, or option is presented until the student enters a response. Response latency data is often used to make inferences about how well a student understands a concept. The faster the student answers the question, the better they understand the concept they were being asked about.

The type of data shown in Figures 10.2 and 10.3 provides detailed information on what students are doing as they go through a program. This kind of data should be collected during pilot testing of a program to determine what revisions are needed. Most authoring software has built-in capabilities to collect such data. However, it's up to you to make use of it.

Make revisions according to a plan, not haphazardly

Because of the branching structure, making revisions in a program is more complicated than in a linear media such as print or video. Branching introduces a lot of interdependencies among different parts of a course or lesson. For example, the scores from a pre-test taken at the beginning of the program may be used within each lesson to determine what information to present or skip. Changes to one part of a program are likely to affect other parts because of the interdependencies.

For this reason, it is important not to make revisions in a haphazard manner. When making a change to a specific sequence in a program, the storyboard corresponding to that sequence should be checked to see what other sequences will be affected and may need to be changed. A revision log should be kept that lists all changes made to a program, when they were made, who made them, and why. When problems appear as a result of changes, the revision log is very useful in tracking down what happened.

It is also important to group changes into successive versions or releases of a program rather than make the changes continuously. When a new version or release of a program is distributed, it will contain all the changes made since the previous version or release. Each new version should completely replace the previous one to prevent conflicts or confusion between the updated and current versions. In fact, instructions with the new release usually specify that the old version should be thrown away.

By releasing all new changes together, it is possible to check the interaction among changes to make sure that there are no conflicts. Sometimes two changes that work fine by themselves will not work together (because they accidentally use the same files or variables). Each version must be checked and tested as a complete program.

The frequency of new releases should be dictated by the number and significance of the changes made. During the introduction phase of a new program, it is not uncommon to distribute a new version every month or two since there are typically many changes needed in the beginning. Once a course becomes mature, new versions are likely to be needed much less frequently (e.g., every six months or annually).

Collect attitude data as well as response data

One thing that is easy to forget when designing instructional programs is that they work better if students like them. For this reason, it is important to collect attitudinal data as well as response data during pilot testing. Table 10.4 lists examples of the type of questions that can be asked to find out if students like a program. Normally these questions would be phrased so that the student can agree or

Table 10.4   *Examples of Attitudinal Questions*

1. Did you find this lesson interesting? Why / Why not?
2. Would you recommend this course to a friend?
3. Would you have preferred to take this course without using the computer?
4. Were you ever bored while taking this course? When?
5. Did you find this course too long? Too short? About right?
6. Was the content of the course too difficult or too easy? About right?
7. Did the course seem well organized to you? Why not?
8. Were you able to move around in the course as you wanted?
9. Were the screen displays easy to read and understand?

disagree on a five-point scale. Half of the questions would be phrased positively and half negatively to avoid a question set bias. Open response questions should be included too. Students should be asked to explain what they liked and disliked about specific lessons or sequences.

Attitudinal information can be collected in online or offline form. Online data collection has a number of advantages over an offline format. Brief questionnaires can be inserted after each lesson or specific sequences to get the student's immediate reaction. Students may be more candid answering online than offline where a person distributes and collects the questionnaire. The most important advantage to online questionnaires is that the data can be automatically analyzed and summarized by the program, eliminating a manual data entry or calculation step.

Good documentation makes revision easier

In Chapter 3, the importance of design documentation was discussed. Documenting the program itself is also very important. The main value of program documentation is to make revision easier. Things that seem too obvious to write down when the program is written (or were written down on little sheets of yellow paper) tend to become obscure a few months later when a revision is needed. Furthermore, it is very common for the person who makes revisions to a program to be someone different than the person who designed or implemented the program originally.

Table 10.5 lists some of the general things about a program that should be documented. In addition, each unit or sequence in the program should have its own documentation that describes the use of files and variables, subroutines and any special programming techniques.

Almost everyone is in favor of documentation (it's like apple pie and motherhood). However, it's often not done or not done very well. To ensure that it gets done, you must insist that the program is not complete until the documentation is finished. It must be viewed as a critical development task and listed as a step to be completed in the project schedule. In fact, documentation should be designed, developed, tested, and debugged just like the programs that it describes. Testing and debugging is accomplished by having someone other than the original programmer try to understand and make changes to the documented program. It helps to assign responsibility for documentation to a single individual (someone other than the original programmer).

Two classic problems with documentation are that it becomes out of date and gets lost. The same solution can minimize both of these problems: put the documentation in the program itself. If the documentation is included in the program by means of comment statements, it cannot get lost and the chances are much higher that it will get updated when the program does. This makes the program bigger but program size is seldom a problem these days.

Table 10.5   *Program Documentation*

1. Program name, version, and copyright
2. Date of program version and documentation
3. Name and address of developer/programmer
4. Purpose and intended use of program
5. Intended student audience
6. Program duration
7. Required/optional ancillary materials
8. System requirements (memory, peripherals)
9. Program limits
10. References to program design, use, or validation

Summary

This chapter has presented the following guidelines regarding revision

- ☐ Use a checklist to systematically review the quality of a program.
- ☐ Use student response data to find flaws in the instruction.
- ☐ Make revisions according to a plan, not haphazardly.
- ☐ Collect attitude data as well as response data.
- ☐ Good documentation makes revision easier.

APPENDIX: SOURCES OF FURTHER INFORMATION

The preceding chapters have provided a set of guidelines for the design of instructional software. However, this book does not go into depth on the topics discussed nor does it cover many related topics. This Appendix provides additional readings and references.

Design and development of instructional software

The following books discuss the design and development of computer-based instruction. Many of these books also describe the different types of computer-based instruction possible.

Allessi, S. M., & Trollip, S. R. *Computer-Based Instruction: Methods and Development.* Prentice-Hall, Englewood Cliffs, N.J. 1985.

Bork, A. *Learning with Computers.* Digital Press, Bedford, Mass. 1981.

Burke, R. L. *CAI Sourcebook.* Prentice-Hall, Englewood Cliffs, N.J. 1982.

Chambers, J. A., & Sprecher, J. W. *Computer-Assisted Instruction: Its Use in the Classroom.* Spectrum (Prentice-Hall), Englewood Cliffs, N.J. 1983.

Coburn, P., Kelman, P., Roberts, N., Snyder, T., Watt, D., & Weiner, C. *Practical Guide to Computers in Education.* Addison-Wesley, Reading, Mass. 1982.

Dennis, J. R., & Kansky, R. J. *Instructional Computing: An Action Guide for Educators.* Scott, Foresman & Co., Glenview, Ill. 1984.

Godfrey, D., & Sterling, S. *The Elements of CAL.* Reston (Prentice-Hall), Reston, Va. 1982.

Heines, J. M. *Screen Design Strategies for Computer-Assisted Instruction*. Digital Press, Bedford, Mass. 1984.

Hunter, B. *My Students Use Computers*. Reston (Prentice-Hall), Reston, Va. 1983.

Kearsley, G. *Computer Based Training: A Guide to Selection and Implementation*. Addison-Wesley, Reading, Mass. 1983.

Landa, R. K. *Creating Courseware: A Beginner's Guide*. Harper & Row, N.Y. 1984.

Lathrop, A., & Goodson, B. *Courseware in the Classroom: Selecting, Organizing, and Using Educational Software*. Addison-Wesley, Reading, Mass. 1983.

O'Neil, H. F. ed. *Computer-Based Instruction: A State of the Art Assessment*. Academic Press, N.Y. 1981.

Papert, S. *Mindstorms: Children, Computers and Powerful Ideas*. Basic Books, N.Y. 1980.

Steinberg, E. *Teaching Computers to Teach*. Erlbaum, Hillsdale, N.J. 1984.

Walker, D. F., & Hess, R. D. *Instructional Software: Principles and Perspectives for Design and Use*. Wadsworth, Belmont, Calif. 1984.

Instructional design

Good quality instruction depends upon the use of instructional design principles and techniques. The following sources cover these principles.

Fleming, M., & Levie, W.H. *Instructional Message Design: Principles from the Behavioral Sciences*. Educational Technology Publications, Englewood Cliffs, N.J. 1978.

Gagne, R. M., & Briggs, L. J. *Principles of Instructional Design*. Holt, Rinehart & Winston, N.Y. 1979.

Journal of Instructional Development. Association for Educational Communications and Technology, Washington, D.C.

Merrill, M. D., & Tennyson, R. D. *Teaching Concepts: An Instructional Design Guide*. Educational Technology Publications, Englewood Cliffs, N.J. 1977.

O'Neil, H. F., ed. *Procedures for Instructional Systems Development*. Academic Press, N.Y. 1979.

Reigeluth, C. M., ed. *Instructional Design Theories and Models: An Overview of Their Current Status.* Erlbaum, Hillsdale, N.J. 1983.

Zemke, R., & Kramlinger, T. *Figuring Things Out: A Trainer's Guide to Needs and Task Analysis.* Addison-Wesley, Reading, Mass. 1982.

Other media

The following references cover the design of other media as it relates to interactive software.

Daynes, R., & Butler, B. *The Videodisc Book.* Wiley & Sons, N.Y. 1984.

DeBloois, M. *Videodisc/Microcomputer Courseware Design.* Educational Technology Publications, Englewood Cliffs, N.J. 1982.

Gayeski, D., & Williams, D. *Interactive Media.* Prentice-Hall, Englewood Cliffs, N.J. 1985.

Howard, J. "What Is Good Documentation?" *Byte,* March 1981.

Jonassen, D. H. *The Technology of Text.* Educational Technology Publications, Englewood Cliffs, N.J. 1982.

Laird, D. & House, R. *Interactive Classroom Instruction.* Scott, Foresman & Co., Glenview, Ill. 1985.

McGehee, B. M. *Writing Software User Manuals.* Writer's Digest Books, Cincinnati, Oh. 1984.

Simulations and games

Simulations and games represent one of the most powerful forms of instructional software because they really exploit the interactive capability of computers. Here are some sources of further information on the design of simulations or games.

Boocock, S. S., & Schild, E. O., eds. *Simulation Games in Learning.* Sage, Beverly Hills, CA. 1968.

Crawford, C. *The Art of Computer Game Design.* Osborne/McGraw-Hill, Berkeley, Calif. 1984.

Ellington, H., Adinall, E., & Percival, F. *A Handbook of Game Design.* Kogan Page, London, U.K. 1982.

Horn, R., & Cleaves, A. *The Guide to Simulations/Games for Education and Training.* Sage, Beverly Hills, Calif. 1980.

Malone, T. "What Makes Computer Games Fun?" *Byte,* December 1981.

Simulation and Games: An International Journal of Theory, Design, and Research. Sage, Beverly Hills, Calif.

Thiagarajan, S., & Stolovitch, H. D. *Instructional Simulation Games.* Educational Technology Publications, Englewood Cliffs, N.J. 1978.

Authoring software

As discussed in Chapter 1, authoring software can make a significant difference in the development of instructional software. The following sources discuss authoring software.

Guide to Computer Based Training. Weingarten Publications, Inc., Boston, Mass. 1985.

Kearsley, G. "Authoring Systems in Computer Based Education." *Communications of the ACM* (July 1982): 429–437.

Kearsley, G. "Authoring Tools: An Introduction." *Journal of Computer Based Instruction.* Special Issue on Authoring Software. (Summer 1984): 1.

Locatis, C. & Carr, V. "Selecting Authoring Systems." *Journal of Computer Based Instruction* (Spring 1985): 28–33.

Starkweather, J. *A User's Guide to PILOT.* Spectrum (Prentice-Hall), Englewood Cliffs, N.J. 1985.

Programming techniques

The development of quality instructional software depends upon the use of good programming methods. Here are some recommended books on programming techniques.

Kernighan, B., & Plauger, P. *Elements of Programming Style.* McGraw-Hill, N.Y. 1978.

Knuth, D. E. *The Art of Computer Programming, vol. 1.* Addison-Wesley, Reading, Mass. 1973.

Mack, B. & Heath, P., eds. *Guide to Good Programming.* Halsted Press, N.Y. 1980.

Martin, J., & McClure, C. *Diagramming Techniques for Analysts and Programmers*. Prentice-Hall, Englewood Cliffs, N.J. 1985.
Ledgard, H. F. *Programming Proverbs*. Hayden, Rochelle Park, N.J. 1975.
Van Tassel, D. *Program Style, Design, Efficiency, Debugging and Testing*. Prentice-Hall, Englewood Cliffs, N.J. 1974.
Yourdon, E. *Techniques of Program Structure and Design*. Prentice-Hall, Englewood Cliffs, N.J. 1975.

Human factors of computing

Human factors engineering is concerned with the design of effective human-machine interfaces. In recent years, a lot of attention has been given to human-computer interfaces as discussed in the following books.

Badre, A., & Shneiderman, B. *Directions in Human-Computer Interaction*. Ablex, Norwood, N.J. 1982.
Card, S., Moran, T. P., & Newell, A. *The Psychology of Human-Computer Interaction*. Erlbaum, Hillsdale, N.J. 1983.
Heckel, P. *The Elements of Friendly Software Design*. Warner, N.Y. 1982.
Martin, J. *Design of Man-Computer Dialogues*. Prentice-Hall, Englewood Cliffs, N.J. 1973.
Shneiderman, B. *Software Psychology*. Winthrop, Cambridge, Mass. 1980.
Thomas, J. C., & Schneider, M. *Human Factors in Computing Systems*. Ablex, Norwood, N.J. 1984.

Helps

As discussed in Chapter 8, helps represent an important form of embedded training. Here are some articles that specifically discuss help systems.

Carroll, J. M., & Carrithers, C. "Training Wheels in a User Interface." *Communications of the ACM* (August 1984): 800–806.
Houghton, R. C. "Online Help Systems: A Conspectus." *Communications of the ACM*. February 1984, 128–133.

Stone, D., et al. "Hypertext as a Component in a Computer Based Technical Information System." *Journal of Computer Based Instruction* (Spring 1983).

Wilensky, R., Avens, Y., & Chin, D. "Talking to UNIX in English: An Overview of UC." *Communications of the ACM* (June 1984): 574–593.

Artificial Intelligence

Artificial Intelligence (AI) is concerned with the development of programs that exhibit intelligent capabilities such as inference, reasoning, and understanding. AI programming techniques are necessary to develop sophisticated instructional software. The following books outline AI concepts.

Harmon, P., & King, D. *Expert Systems: Artificial Intelligence in Business.* Wiley & Sons, N.Y. 1985.

King, D., ed. *Parsing Natural Language.* Academic Press, N.Y. 1983.

O'Shea, T., & Self, J. *Learning and Teaching with Computers: Artificial Intelligence in Education.* Prentice-Hall, Englewood Cliffs, N.J. 1983.

Sleeman, D., & Brown, J. S. *Intelligent Tutoring Systems.* Academic Press, N.Y. 1982.

Winograd, T. *Understanding Natural Language.* Academic Press, N.Y. 1972.

Winston, P. *Artificial Intelligence.* Addison-Wesley, Reading, Mass. 1984.

Exemplary instructional software

The proof of the pudding with respect to the design of instructional software is quality programs. Here is a list of commercially available programs that run on different personal computers and exemplify good design features.

Bank Street Writer, Scholastic Inc. Jefferson City, Mo. A word processing program specifically designed for teaching young children how to use word processing.

Conquering Stress. KJ Software, Phoenix, Ariz. One of the programs from the "DAVID Noted Author Series," which are based upon the works of well-known authors in different subject areas.

Elementary My Apple, Apple Computer Co., Cupertino, Calif. This diskette contains Darts, an arithmetic drill, Lemonade, a "business" game, and Shell Games, a test creation program.

Flight Simulator, Microsoft Corp., Bellevue, Wash. This program is a good illustration of a procedural simulation (practice flying an airplane).

Leading Effectively, Thoughtware Inc., Coconut Grove, Fla. One in a series of diagnostic programs that lets you assess your business and interpersonal skills.

Operation: Frog. Scholastic Inc. Jefferson City, Mo. A program that simulates the dissection of a frog.

Master Type, Scarborough Systems, Tarrytown, N.Y. One of the more popular typing drill programs that uses an action game format.

Personal Filing System (PFS), Software Publishing Co., Mountainview, Calif. A series of easy-to-use data management programs widely used in schools. Scholastic Inc. publishes a series of educational databases that can be used with PFS programs.

President Elect. Strategic Simulations, Palo Alto, Calif. A simulation of a presidential election that uses historical databases for authentic predictions.

The Print Shop, Broderbund Software Inc., San Raphael, Calif. A simple graphics design program that includes a library of "clip art."

Rocky's Boots, The Learning Company, Portola, Calif. A problem-solving program that teaches logic concepts.

Sold!, Courseware Inc., San Diego, Calif. A sales call simulation game with a built-in sales call planner.

Spellicopter, Designware Inc., San Francisco, Calif. A spelling drill with an interesting game format and the capability to choose levels and add new words.

Stickybear Math, Weekly Reader Family Software (Xerox), Stamford, Conn. An arithmetic drill with an adventure theme and good graphics. One of a series.

Story Maker, Spinnaker Software, Boston, Mass. A program that allows students to make up stories and illustrate them.

The Management Edge, Human Edge Software, Palo Alto, Calif. One of a series of diagnostic programs that allow you to assess your business and interpersonal skills.

Where In the World Is Carmen Sandiego?, Broderbund Software Inc., San Raphael, Calif. A geography program that is accompanied by the World Almanac.

GLOSSARY

This glossary explains important concepts and terms used in the design of instructional software.

Animation: Movement of a graphic across the screen. Can be used to show dynamic processes or for visual effects. Involves rapid display and erasure of a graphic with a slight change in screen location each time.

Application Software: Programs that perform some sort of application, such as word processing, database retrieval, calculations (i.e., spreadsheet), graphics design, etc.

Bit-Map: A type of display in which every picture element (pixel) can be addressed. Contrasts with raster scan type display in which only complete lines can be addressed. Bit-mapped displays allow much higher resolution text and graphics.

Branching: The control of sequence in a program.

Bugs: Errors in programs that prevent them from working as intended.

Computerese: Technical computer terminology.

Cursor: A marker that indicates the location on the screen of the next input. The marker is usually a blinking square, line, or arrow. The cursor can be moved via arrow keys or some kind of pointing device (e.g., mouse, trackball).

Data: Any information used by a program or stored on a disk.

Debugging: The process of finding and fixing bugs in a program.

Disk: The storage medium for program and files. Is read by and written to by a disk drive. (Disks are synonymous with diskettes.)

Editor: A special type of program that lets you enter and modify text, graphics, or other options.

Feedback: Messages generated as a result of a user response.

File: Information (data) stored on a disk and identified by a unique name for subsequent retrieval.

Flow Chart: A diagram that shows the logic flow (branching) of a program.

Function Keys: Special keys provided on the keyboard which have no fixed function. Their function is defined by a program and can be changed as often as desired.

Hardware: The physical components of a computer system (e.g., monitor, disk drives, printers).

Icons: Visual symbols used to represent options or data (e.g., a symbol of a trash can represents deletion of a file).

Mouse: An input device used on some computers to move the cursor. The mouse is a small box that can be rolled on a flat surface. The movement of the cursor on the screen matches the movement of the mouse.

Overlay: To display one thing on top of another, usually by adding something to the original display.

Parser: A program that translates or decodes a symbolic or natural language sequence.

Peripherals: Input, output, or storage devices (hardware) such as a mouse, printer, or disk drive.

Pixel: The smallest point that can be addressed on a display screen (abbreviation for picture element).

Pop-up/Pull-down: A window or menu that overlays the current display when it is selected from an option list. When an option is selected from the menu or when the window is closed, it disappears.

Scrolling: Moving the top lines off the screen each time something new is entered at the bottom. Contrasts with paging, in which entire screens are replaced.

Software: The programs that make a computer do something.

Subroutine: A self-contained program that can be called by the main program.

Variables: Labels given to values in a program which can change.

Vector: An ordered list of numbers.

Viewports: *See* windows.

Windows: Defining a portion of the screen for display. Overlapping windows are displayed on top of the current display.

INDEX